Praise for
MAIN STREET BOOM:
Uncovering the Generational Gold Mine
and Xavier Egan

"As someone who has experienced the transformative power of strategic business acquisitions firsthand, I can confidently say that 'Main Street Boom: Uncovering the Generational Gold Mine' is an essential read for any aspiring entrepreneur. Xavier Egan's insights into identifying and unlocking the hidden potential in small businesses resonate deeply with my journey in the liquor industry.

Through acquiring and expanding a company, I was able to significantly grow my business, ultimately leading to a successful sale to a larger provider. Egan's guidance on spotting, evaluating, and acquiring businesses is spot-on and invaluable. This book is a goldmine of practical strategies and inspirational stories that will empower you to achieve your entrepreneurial dreams. Don't miss out on the opportunity to learn from one of the best in the business."

— **Jimmy Gaston, CEO,**
Premiere 360

Main Stream Boom is a refreshing perspective in a world where increasing awareness can be a game changer. Xavier accomplishes this with insight and experience. He helps those select owners and advisors see further to impact their lives and legacy. This is a must read if you want to increase enterprise value, readiness and attractiveness; kudos on this awesome work!

— **Akili Johnson,** SE-AWMA®, CEPA®, CPFA®
Dallas Chapter President, Exit Planning Institute

cheezMEDIA

MAIN STREET BOOM

Copyright Notice for "Main Street Boom: Uncovering the Generational Gold Mine" by Cheez Media LLC.

Copyright © 2024 by Cheez Media LLC. All rights reserved. Printed in the United States of America. Except as permitted under the United States Copyright Act of 1976, no part of this publication may be reproduced or distributed in any form or by any means, or stored in a database or retrieval system, including photocopying, recording, or other electronic or mechanical methods, without the prior written permission of the author, except in the case of brief quotations embodied in critical reviews and specific other noncommercial uses permitted by copyright law. For permission requests, write to the publisher, addressed "Attention: Cheez Media Coordinator," at the address below.

Publisher

cheezMEDIA

2000 E. Lamar Blvd. Ste 510
Arlington, TX. 76006

ISBN: 979-8-9911259-0-1 (Paperback)
ISBN: 979-8-9911259-3-2 (Hardcopy)

Foreword by David Mullings, Chairman & CEO, Blue Mahoe Holdings, Inc.
Afterword by Sam Mattox, Managing Partner, YSCO
Editor in Chief & Cover Design Illustrator: Syreeta Mitchell
Author Photograph by Tavia Whitlowe

Special discounts for bulk sales are available.
Please contact info@makecheez.com.

Disclaimer

The information provided in "Main Street Boom: Uncovering the Generational Gold Mine" by Xavier Egan is for general informational purposes only. The author and publisher make no representation or warranties concerning the accuracy, applicability, fitness, or completeness of the contents of this book. They disclaim any warranties (expressed or implied), merchantability, or fitness for any particular purpose. The author and publisher shall not be held liable for any loss or other damages, including but not limited to special, incidental, consequential, or other damages.

As always, the advice of a competent legal, tax, accounting, or other professional should be sought. The author and publisher do not warrant the performance, effectiveness, or applicability of any sites listed or linked to this book.

Short List of What This Book Does NOT Provide:

1. Personalized financial advice or legal consultation.
2. Guarantee of success in business ventures or investments.
3. Endorsement of specific business strategies as foolproof.
4. Assurance that the historical examples or case studies will replicate in current times.
5. A one-size-fits-all solution for business or investment issues.

Readers should be aware that the strategies and examples contained in this book are not intended as a promise or guarantee of earnings. Your success in attaining the results claimed in this book depends on the time you devote to the ideas and techniques mentioned, your finances, knowledge, and various skills.

cheezMEDIA

MAIN STREET BOOM

UNCOVERING THE GENERATIONAL GOLD MINE

XAVIER EGAN

To my incredible family:
For my beloved wife, my amazing son and daughter,
and my entrepreneurial family.

Your unwavering love, encouragement, and inspiration
have been the backbone of my journey.
This book is as much yours
as it is mine.

CONTENTS

	FOREWORD	XII
	PREFACE	XIII
Chapter 1	The Main Street Effect	1
Chapter 2	The New Frontier of Generational Wealth Transfer	11
Chapter 3	Good, Better, Best	27
Chapter 4	Entrepreneurship is Hard	37
Chapter 5	Suitability	43
Chapter 6	Fundability	55
Chapter 7	Identifying Deal Partners	65
Chapter 8	Digging for Gold	75
Chapter 9	Acquisition Advantage	83
Chapter 10	Main Street Case Studies	101
Chapter 11	Grow Baby Grow	119
	AFTERWORD	133
	AUTHOR'S NOTE	137
	DEFINITIONS	139
	REFERENCES	146

FOREWORD

It is commonly said today that over 10,000 Baby Boomers retire each day and will do for the foreseeable future. We are witnessing the greatest transfer of wealth between two generations and most Boomer Business Owners have children who do not want to run the family business. This means that these owners need an exit.

We do not choose when we are born or where we are born but you are lucky to be able to take advantage of the many opportunities to buy an existing, profitable business that you can modernize and scale. Xavier Egan painstakingly lays out the actual steps to find and buy Main Street businesses. This book will guide you and share the unvarnished truth about what it takes.

As a student of Warren Buffett and Michael Lee-Chin, I strongly believe in the idea that it is better to own a piece of an existing business domiciled in a strong, long-term growth industry that prudently manages money and then hold it for the long-term. Baby Boomer business owners created their wealth by building such businesses and Xavier gives you the recipe that allows you to take them over.

I guarantee that you will also buy copies to give to anyone interested in getting into business because you will see that it is easier to raise capital to buy an existing business than to start your own. Enjoy the excellent guidebook written by Xavier and remember to pay it forward after you do well.

David P. A. Mullings, Chairman and CEO
Blue Mahoe Holdings, Inc.

PREFACE

I always wanted to be an entrepreneur when I grew up. As a kid, I thought I would become a doctor or a lawyer, like many of my friends. But then I chose dentistry, because it seemed like a good way to start my own business. I liked the idea of having my own practice, setting my own hours, and living the way I wanted. In high school, I joined a medical program that let me try different jobs in the hospital. I was lucky to get a chance to work in the cancer department of a big research hospital. But when I saw a doctor treating a patient with a big tumor, I knew medicine was not for me. I felt a bit queasy and was unable to offer much assistance.

As a result, I decided to enroll in business school after graduating from high school. I was always drawn to entrepreneurship and understood that being employed was only a temporary solution. Gaining practical experience in various industries was crucial to learn and grow as an entrepreneur. Therefore, I decided to major in accounting, later switching to finance. After completing my degree, I landed a job at a small, privately owned insurance company closely affiliated with my alma mater. This job provided me with a remarkable opportunity to gain a thorough understanding of the insurance business. The company was insuring a massive stadium in the city, and I was astounded by how a small team of four or five people could reap millions of dollars' worth of business.

Growing up, my parents exposed me to the world of entrepreneurship. My mother worked in corporate America while pursuing entrepreneurial ventures, such as tax preparation and sewing. On the other hand, my father was a transportation entrepreneur who dabbled in various businesses, including owning trucks, vending machines, and restaurants. Their experiences, combined with my own, fueled my passion for entrepreneurship.

The story recounted by my father involves his vending machine business, where he brought home the coins and asked for my assistance, as a young child, to wrap some of the coins for deposit at the bank. Looking at the table full of currency, I asked what's my "cut", which prompted my father to remark that he recognized my potential as a businessman. Fast forward to my college years, where I was given an excellent opportunity to learn about accounting and finance, which became my business language. Upon entering the business world, I discovered that small-scale operations could significantly impact building activities, with the owners reaping the majority of the benefits. This realization was an eye-opening experience, and I continued to seek out similar entrepreneurial spaces.

After a few jobs, I ventured into consulting, where I was considered an elf on the shelf, responsible for handling backlog issues and assisting with serious contracts. One day, a Department of Defense contractor contacted the consulting team, seeking assistance with their workload. They requested the most capable individual to take charge of the project, and the consulting company assigned me to the task. I was astounded to learn that the company was worth two billion dollars when I joined, and by the time I left, it had grown to five billion dollars, with a global presence and over ten thousand employees in multiple countries.

This experience proved to be an excellent opportunity to learn and understand the intricacies of the business world, with private companies capable of generating billions of dollars in revenue. It reinforced the notion that even small teams could significantly impact business activities, provided they had the right inputs and outputs in place.

In addition to my corporate activities, I have been involved in several business ventures. I have established a couple of consulting companies and invested in real estate, owning a block of a street in Dallas where the tenants on the left side paid us rent. However, the cash flow needed to be increased, and the consistency of starting a business was challenging, leading me to explore different avenues.

In pursuit of financial stability, I ventured into purchasing a company with no down payment, a strategy similar to real estate investment. The venture was profitable, generating $40,000 to $50,000 monthly revenue. However, it was unstable, prompting me to shift to new markets. Despite the shift, I maintained my workforce in accounting and finance while ascending corporate-wise to CFO of global business units, managing hundreds of millions of dollars and supporting various firms across different countries.

Entrepreneurship has always been my passion, and I sought to explore different ways to pursue it. My tenure in a DoD contracting company that generated billions of dollars in revenue was a significant learning experience. I rose through the ranks, and some high-ranking personalities approached me due to my reporting to the board of directors and shareholders.

The sensitivity of the projects I was working on drew attention, and some gentlemen visited my office, which was surprising considering the building's security protocols.

I discovered that the company was part of a $50 billion private equity portfolio, a realization that opened my mind to different entrepreneurship strategies. Although their strategy was on a large scale, my goal was to learn how to deploy similar skills to achieve my ambitions.

Upon reviewing their portfolio, I was struck that the companies in question did not conform to the traditional investment patterns. Commonly, individuals tend to invest in areas that align with their expertise or interests - for example, tech or oil. However, the companies in this portfolio exhibited no fundamental commonalities between them. Further investigation revealed that their cash flow was the common thread connecting these companies. Moreover, the portfolio managers possessed a keen business sense, recognizing that minor improvements could further boost cash flow. These observations led me to realize that adopting a private equity mentality could enable me to acquire and grow businesses at scale, reaching the $50 billion mark and beyond.

As I tried to apply this insight in my early career, I bought a company when I was 23 or 24 years old. Sadly, this venture was not successful. But with better knowledge, I did not give up on this goal and used the resources I had gained from my transition to corporate America. The first two companies I bought gave me cash flow and valuable life lessons but did not meet my goals for scalability and personal growth. The third company I acquired was a Main Street M & A or business brokerage, which helped people across the country sell their businesses through effective marketing. This turned out to be the ideal fit for me.

Through my experiences in buying and running companies, I learned the importance of developing financial stewardship and gaining a deeper understanding of making deals and transactions. At the level of Main Street brokerage, this could be done at scale, enabling a more comprehensive range of individuals to participate in the transfer of businesses. My passion for entrepreneurship and desire to share the knowledge I have gained motivated me to write this book. I want to inspire others to take advantage of the opportunities available, regardless of their financial resources.

By opportunities, I mean the hidden treasures that await you in the Main Street market. This is where you can find businesses that generate steady cash flow, have loyal customers, and offer room for improvement. These are the businesses that most people overlook or undervalue, but they are the ones that can make you rich. In this book, I will show you how to spot, evaluate, and acquire these gems, and how to make them shine even brighter. You don't need a lot of money, a fancy degree, or a corporate background to do this. You just need the right mindset, the right tools, and the right guidance. That's what I'm here to provide. So, grab your shovel and let's start digging for gold!

Chapter 1
THE MAIN STREET EFFECT

Small businesses are like hidden treasures waiting to be discovered. They may not look like much on the surface, but they hold immense value and potential for those who know how to find and unlock them. We will explore the Main Street market, where you can find these gems and how to make them shine even brighter. You will learn how to spot, evaluate, and acquire these businesses, and how to grow and diversify them. This is where real wealth is created, and where you can achieve your entrepreneurial dreams. So, grab your pickaxe and let's start digging for gold!

Exploring the Business Market

The Baby Boomer generation, who are now reaching retirement age, own a significant number of small businesses that could provide a gold mine of wealth for the newer generation. As the Baby Boomers get closer to retiring, they are considering their options for handing down their businesses to the younger generation. This opens up a great chance for the younger generation to inherit a thriving business that has already established a name.

Small businesses come in all shapes and sizes and are the backbone of the economy, often serving as the lifeblood of their local communities. These businesses, run by individual captains, embody the entrepreneurial dream, showcasing the notion that one person can make a difference. They are agile, able to adapt and pivot quickly in response to the changing market trends and consumer needs. With fewer than 20 employees, these businesses are often tight-knit and efficient, and they can operate with lean budgets.

Understanding the nuances of the market, including the potential for strategic alliances and acquisitions, can help businesses unlock new levels of success and profitability, providing a pathway for growth and diversification.

While small businesses are a vital part of the market, public companies play a significant role in setting standards and trends for smaller businesses to follow or differentiate themselves from. Public companies are often larger and have a more significant financial backing, which allows them to invest in research and development, marketing, and other areas that smaller businesses may not be able to afford. However, smaller businesses have an advantage in that they are more agile and can adapt more quickly to changes in the market.

Knowing the market's subtleties, such as the possibilities for alliances and acquisitions, can help businesses reach new heights of success and profit. For instance, a business can grow, diversify, and gain an advantage by merging or acquiring another business. A partnership with another business can also help succeed, by sharing resources and knowledge.

What is Main Street?

Main Street businesses are like a wealth explosion waiting to happen. They may seem small and insignificant, but together they represent a massive force that drives the economy forward. In fact, they make up a staggering 99.9% of all businesses in the United States. Their impact on the Gross Domestic Product (GDP) cannot be overstated, as they contribute significantly to the nation's economic output and provide employment opportunities that form the backbone of the American workforce.

Just like an explosion, the distribution of these enterprises is diverse and wide-ranging. Of the 33.2 million in the US, there are 27.1 million businesses that operate without any employees, fueled by self-starters and independent contractors who embody the spirit of autonomy and freedom. These businesses represent the spark that ignites the explosion. Then there are 5.4 million businesses that have between 1 and 18 employees, often tight-knit teams that operate like families, sharing triumphs and challenges alike. These businesses represent the kindling that fuels the explosion. Finally, there are 650,000 businesses with 20 to 499 employees, mini powerhouses that maintain a delicate balance between the nimble agility of small firms and the robust processes of larger corporations. These businesses represent the explosive force that propels the economy forward.

Small businesses cover the gamut from corner stores to tech startups, each with unique stories of innovation, perseverance, and resilience. They are the center of our communities, fueling local economies and providing essential services. From the local bakery that wakes up before dawn to prepare the freshest bread in town to the small tech firm developing cutting-edge software, small businesses feed our communities in more ways than one.

However, the journey of a small business is not without its challenges. They face many hurdles, from securing funding and navigating regulatory landscapes to competing with larger companies that wield greater resources. Yet, despite these challenges, Main Street continues to thrive, driven by passion, creativity, and an unyielding spirit of entrepreneurship.

Small businesses are the faces of our neighbors, friends, and family members who pour their hearts into their work. They understand their local communities' needs and are nimble enough to adapt quickly to changing market dynamics. Moreover, small businesses are incubators for innovation. They are often the birthplace of groundbreaking ideas that transform industries. Their size allows them to take risks and pivot in ways that larger companies cannot, making them essential players in the economy's booming growth.

Unfortunately, the COVID-19 pandemic has been like a dampener on this explosion. Small and local businesses have faced significant challenges, such as reduced foot traffic and sales, operational difficulties, financial hardships, reliance on government support, and an impact on the community. However, like an eruption that is temporarily dampened, small businesses are resilient and will continue to grow and thrive in the years to come.

Main Street Influence

Let's talk about the force of nearly 60 million individuals employed by small businesses. These employees make up about 47.1% of the total private-sector workforce, which is no small feat. These individuals are the faces behind the counters, the minds behind the services, and the hands crafting the products that we rely on every day. Their contributions are more than just economic figures; they represent the aspirations and achievements of real people making a tangible impact on our lives.

Small businesses are not just local corner shops or cafes; they are also technology startups, consulting firms, and manufacturing plants. Among them, 23% have contracts with public and municipal bodies, embedding these enterprises into the very fabric of our society and governance. This relationship is symbiotic, with small businesses providing innovative solutions to public needs while receiving a steady stream of business that supports their growth and stability.

When we talk about the economy, we often hear the term 'Gross Domestic Product' or GDP. Small businesses contribute an astonishing 44% to the U.S. GDP. This is almost half of the nation's economic output, originating from the diverse array of small-scale operations that dot the American landscape. They are not just part of the economy; they are a driving force that propels it.

Moreover, employing 46.4% of the workforce is a testament to the vital role small businesses play in job creation. They are often the first to hire, providing opportunities for entry-level workers, seasoned professionals, and everyone in between. These businesses are flexible, able to adjust to market shifts, and can act as a springboard for the future's industry leaders.

So, what does this all mean for you, the reader? It means that whether you're an entrepreneur, a consumer, a policy-maker, or simply an engaged citizen, you play a part in this ecosystem. If you run a small business, you're at the forefront of a powerful movement that shapes our economy. As a consumer, when you choose to support local businesses, you're casting a vote for a vibrant and diverse marketplace.

For policymakers, understanding the importance of small businesses means creating an environment where they can thrive—through supportive legislation, accessible financing options, and opportunities for growth. And for citizens, it's about recognizing the value these businesses bring to your communities and advocating for their success.

In essence, the narrative of small business is one of empowerment, opportunity, and resilience. They show us that with passion, hard work, and a bit of ingenuity, anyone can make a significant impact. They demonstrate that success is not measured solely by the size of a company but by the strength of its ideas and the commitment to its people.

The main street narrative is also about the future. With every new startup, with every innovative product, and with each service rendered, small businesses are rewriting the script of what's possible. They're setting the stage for a more dynamic, more inclusive economy where the big dreams of small businesses can indeed become big realities.

Business: The Core of Economics

Picture this: 65% of these ventures are profitable, a testament to the ingenuity and resilience of those at the top. Among these, a notable 9% have crossed the threshold into a realm where they command earnings of over $1 million. These figures are not just statistics; they are stories of success, of overcoming odds, and of the relentless pursuit of growth.

Despite such profitability, the majority of small business owners, over 86% to be precise, draw a yearly salary of less than $100,000. This is a clear indicator that, for many, the entrepreneurial journey is not just about financial gain but is also driven by deeper motivations and commitments. It's about creating value, fostering community, and building something that stands the test of time.

The dedication of small business owners is further highlighted by the fact that 19% of them work more than 60 hours a week. This is not just a number; it's a representation of early mornings, late nights, and sacrificed weekends. It's a display of commitment that separates the dreamers from the doers, the entrepreneurs who are willing to invest not just their money but their time and life into their vision.

If you have an entrepreneurial spirit and want to start your own venture, you might be wondering what motivates people to launch a business. Here are some common reasons for becoming an entrepreneur:

1. **Being Their Own Boss (60% of business owners):** This reflects the journey of digging for gold, much like a miner who ventures into the unknown. It's about having the freedom to explore, discover, and create, without being constrained by someone else's rules or expectations. These entrepreneurs are motivated by autonomy, much like a miner who follows his own instincts, guided by his own maps, driven by his own passion.

2. **Leaving the Corporate Grind (47%):** This reflects the journey of seeking new opportunities, much like a prospector who leaves behind the comfort and security of his home to join the gold rush. It's about venturing

into unknown territories (entrepreneurship) to find new sources of wealth and value, driven by a desire to strike gold rather than settling for a fixed income.

3. **Driven by Passion (31%):** This is similar to a contagious excitement that spreads among those who hear about the riches of the gold fields. It's like a spark that ignites a fire, motivating one to take action and join the adventure. These entrepreneurs are driven by their passion, much like a prospector who risks everything to find gold, driven by a vision of a better future that is worth pursuing.

Each of these motivations reflects a different aspect of the entrepreneurial spirit, embodying the essence of the "Boom" theme – the powerful drive to start something new, break free from constraints, and follow one's own path with passion and determination.

Now, imagine a world where the strategy of mergers and acquisitions (M&A) is not just for the corporate giants but is also the best strategy for these Main Street businesses. Buying cash flow becomes not just a tactic but a strategic move that can catapult a business into new realms of success. An acquisition strategy can offer a fast track to growth, an expansion of capabilities, and an edge over the competition.

The idea of buying a business that has already shown success and generates income can be a huge advantage. It can lead to instant earnings, loyal customers, and a staff that knows how to run the business. This strategy can also expand a business's products and services and reduce risks by distributing them among different sources of income.

When Main Street businesses engage in a takeover, they're not just buying another company; they're buying potential, opportunity, and time. The time that would have otherwise been spent on building something from the ground up can now be invested in scaling and refining the business. Acquiring an existing business can also save time by avoiding the pitfalls and mistakes that often plague new ventures. Instead of learning from trial and error, the buyer can leverage the experience and knowledge of the seller and the existing staff. This can help them avoid costly delays, regulatory hurdles, and customer dissatisfaction. According to a study by the Harvard Business Review, acquisitions can also speed up the time to market by an average of 6.7 months compared to organic growth. This can give the buyer a significant competitive advantage in a fast-changing market.

This can also help them beat their rivals, who may still face difficulties building from zero. By acquiring a proven business model, a loyal customer base, and a skilled workforce, they can accelerate their growth and achieve their goals faster.

For the entrepreneur willing to take this path, the rewards can be substantial. But it's not without its challenges. The process of identifying the right business to acquire, conducting due diligence, negotiating a deal, and then integrating into the new company requires skill, patience, and a strategic mindset.

But dreams are not enough to sustain a business. Entrepreneurship also entails risks, challenges, and hardships that can test the resolve of even the most passionate and determined individuals. Starting a business from scratch is a daunting task, requiring a combination of skills, resources, and luck that few possess. It can take years of hard work, sacrifice, and perseverance to build a successful enterprise, and many fail along the way. According to the U.S. Bureau of Labor Statistics, about 20% of new businesses fail within the first year, and only about half survive past the fifth year. The odds are even worse for innovative startups, which face more uncertainty and competition than established businesses.

Is there a better way to pursue the entrepreneurial dream? Is there a shortcut to the goal, a faster and safer route to the gold? For some entrepreneurs, the answer is yes: acquisition. Rather than starting from zero, they choose to buy an existing business that already has a proven track record, a loyal customer base, and a skilled workforce.

Acquisition can be a powerful strategy to achieve the entrepreneurial dream, but it requires a different set of skills, resources, and mindset than starting a business from scratch. Whether you are a seasoned entrepreneur looking for a new opportunity, a first-time buyer seeking to enter the world of business ownership, or a corporate executive looking for a strategic acquisition, this book will provide you with the tools and guidance you need to succeed in the game.

Chapter 2
THE NEW FRONTIER OF GENERATIONAL WEALTH TRANSFER

We are living in an unprecedented time of change and opportunity. A massive amount of wealth and business value is about to be unleashed, creating a new frontier for entrepreneurs and investors. This is the generational wealth transfer, the largest shift in ownership and assets that the world has ever seen.

This is not a mere transfer; it's a transformation. It's a chance to reinvent, innovate, and revolutionize entire industries and markets. It's a golden opportunity for those who are ready to seize it, to dig deeper, to strike richer, and to claim their stake in the future of business.

But this is also a challenge. It's a test of our ability to adapt, collaborate, and transition. It requires careful planning, strategic thinking, and a vision that spans beyond the horizon. It demands respect for the past and responsibility for the future. It calls for a new generation of leaders who can take the helm and steer the course of the economy and society.

In this book, we'll explore this phenomenon in detail, examining its drivers, dynamics, and implications. We'll look at the current state of the market, the trends and forces shaping the transition, and the opportunities and risks involved.

Whether you're a Baby Boomer looking to sell your business, a Gen Xer or Millennial looking to buy one, or an investor or advisor interested in the market, this book will equip you with the knowledge, skills, and tools you need to succeed in the new frontier of generational wealth transfer. You'll learn how to turn this challenge into an opportunity, how to leverage this transition into a transformation, and how to create lasting value and impact for yourself, your business, and your community.

A New Era of Transition

A modern gold rush is coming. The generational extraction of business value is not just a routine dig; it's a seismic blast reshaping the landscape of the market as we know it. At the core of this change is the Baby Boomer generation—those born between 1946 and 1964—who have been the owners of approximately 40% of small businesses and franchises. This isn't just a rich vein; it's the bedrock of local economies, the source of community wealth, and the spark of entrepreneurial spirit.

As these Baby Boomers approach retirement age, we're staring down the barrel of a $14 trillion transition. Yes, trillion with a 'T.' Over the next five years, this wealth and the associated businesses are set to change hands. This isn't merely a transfer; it's a transformation that holds the potential to redefine markets, introduce new leaders, and ignite a fresh wave of innovation.

But where is this value going? Who are the heirs to this business kingdom? The truth is, the next generation isn't just walking through the door—they're already here. They're the tech-savvy, socially conscious, and global-thinking entrepreneurs. They're the ones who don't just want to inherit a business; they want to reinvent it. They're looking for cash flow, yes, but they're also looking for purpose, sustainability, and impact.

This transition is more than a handover; it's an opportunity. For current owners, it's a chance to cement a legacy, to ensure that the businesses they've poured their lives into continue to thrive. For the incoming wave, it's a platform to build upon, to bring new ideas to the table, and to drive forward with a vision that's as much about values as it is about value.

To illustrate this concept, let's look at an example of a successful generational wealth transfer through business acquisition. Meet Sarah, a 35-year-old entrepreneur who recently acquired a landscaping company from John, a 65-year-old Baby Boomer who was looking to retire. John had built his business over 40 years, serving hundreds of clients and employing dozens of workers. He was proud of his reputation and his loyal customer base, but he also knew that the industry was changing rapidly. He needed to find a successor who could take his business to the next level.

Sarah was the perfect candidate. She had a background in environmental engineering and a passion for sustainable design. She had worked for several years in the corporate sector, managing large-scale projects and leading teams. She wanted to start her own business, but she also wanted to make a positive impact on the environment and the community. She saw an opportunity in John's landscaping company. She approached him with a proposal to buy his business, with the condition that he would stay on as a mentor and advisor for a year. John agreed, impressed by Sarah's enthusiasm and expertise.

The transition was smooth and successful. Sarah retained John's staff and customers, while also introducing new services and technologies. She invested in solar-powered equipment, water-efficient irrigation systems, and organic fertilizers. She expanded the company's offerings to include urban gardening, green roofs, and edible landscapes. She also created a social media presence, a website, and a blog to showcase her work and attract new clients. She increased the company's revenue by 50% in the first year, while also reducing its environmental footprint and enhancing its social impact. John was thrilled to see his business flourish under Sarah's leadership. He felt confident that he had left a lasting legacy and a valuable asset for his family. Sarah was grateful for John's guidance and support. She felt that she had fulfilled her dream of owning a business that aligned with her values and vision.

Let's consider the scope of this shift. Think about your local bakery, the family-run auto repair shop, the independent bookstore that's been around for decades. These aren't just storefronts; they're stories, communities, and livelihoods. Now picture them infused with new energy, new technology, and new business models. Imagine the potential for growth, the opportunities for employment, and the ripple effects through the economy.

This generational shift isn't just a challenge; it's a call to arms. For the Baby Boomers, it's a test of their ability to adapt, to embrace change, and to let go. It requires careful planning, strategic thinking, and a willingness to trust the next generation. For the inheritors, it's about respect for what's come before and a vision for what's ahead. It's about taking the kernel of an idea, a product, or a service and exploding it into something phenomenal. The magnitude of this wealth transfer is not to be underestimated. We're not talking about a simple transaction. We're talking about the future of the marketplace. The businesses that will shape our lives in the coming decades are being decided now—in estate plans, in family discussions, and in the minds of young entrepreneurs ready to take the reins.

What does this mean for you, the reader, the entrepreneur, the investor? It means that the landscape is ripe for the taking. It means there's never been a better time to engage in the market, to seek out opportunities, and to be at the forefront of this generational wave. Whether you're looking to acquire, to sell, or to simply understand the changing face of business, the next few years will be critical.

Setting the Stage for Transition

The Baby Boomer generation has been a formidable force in shaping the economic landscape of the United States. As they approach the twilight of their careers, the impact of their departure will be significant, particularly in the realm of small business and the broader economy. This generation's approach to business succession is setting the stage for one of the largest transitions of economic power in history.

The Baby Boomers' influence is etched deeply into the fabric of the American economy. A staggering three-fourths of Baby Boomer-owned businesses are profitable, a testament to their entrepreneurial spirit and business acumen. This profitability is not just a reflection of successful business practices, but also an indicator of the resilience and adaptability of this generation. Yet, as these titans of industry approach retirement, a pivotal shift is on the horizon. With 70% of business owners aged 50 or older planning to exit their businesses within the next ten years, we're on the cusp of an unprecedented change in the business landscape.

Small businesses, the core of the U.S. economy, generate a remarkable 44% of the country's economic activity. This contribution cannot be understated, as it underscores the importance of ensuring a smooth transition as Baby Boomers step away from their businesses. The continuity of these businesses is crucial; they are not merely establishments, but pillars of local economies, providers of jobs, and incubators of innovation.

As we navigate this turning point, it is essential to consider the methodologies of business succession. Traditional methods may no longer suffice in the face of such a widespread transition. Now is the time for current and prospective business owners to think strategically about mergers and acquisitions (M&A) as a potent strategy for business continuity. Acquisitions offer a pathway for preserving the economic contributions of these businesses, ensuring that their legacy endures and continues to bolster the economy.

Another factor to consider in this transition is the changing preferences and aspirations of the younger generations. Family succession, once a common and expected practice, is no longer a probable option for many Baby Boomer-owned businesses. According to a 2016 survey by PwC, only 23% of family-owned businesses have a robust succession plan in place, and only 18% are confident that the next generation has the skills and drive to take over the business. This suggests a disconnect between the expectations of the current owners and the realities of the successors. Many younger family members may not share the same vision, passion, or interest as their parents. They may have different career goals, values, or lifestyles that are incompatible with running a family business. Rather than forcing a reluctant or unprepared heir to take the helm, it may be more beneficial for both parties to explore other options, such as selling the business to an external buyer or merging with another business. This way, the current owners can ensure a fair return on their investment, while the successors can pursue their own dreams and ambitions.

The question then becomes, how can we facilitate this transition in a way that honors the hard work of the Baby Boomer generation while securing a prosperous future for the next?

As we dig deeper into this new era, it's vital to acknowledge the need for guidance and mentorship. The seasoned wisdom of Baby Boomer business owners is a precious ore that should be mined by the incoming wave of entrepreneurs and investors. This exchange of knowledge and experience is a cornerstone of a successful transition. It ensures that the incoming guardians of these businesses are not just equipped with financial capital but also with the intellectual and social capital necessary to thrive.

Moreover, the transition presents a unique opportunity for innovation. New owners can bring fresh perspectives, technologies, and business models that can drive these businesses to new heights. This fusion of established business practices with innovative approaches can result in a dynamic and revitalized economic sector.

Opportunity in Transition

The demographic reality is stark: people ages 55-plus, who form 20%+ of the U.S. population, own more than half of the small businesses in the United States. This disproportionate ownership signifies an impending seismic shift. As these Baby Boomer entrepreneurs look toward retirement, there is a colossal amount of businesses that will change hands, and herein lies the crux of the opportunity.

Here is a chart that shows the age distribution of the 2023 US population versus the age of business owners:

Age Group	% of US Population	% of Business Owners
Under 35	46.0%	6%
35-44	12.5%	22%
45-54	12.6%	21%
55-64	13.1%	28%
65+	15.8%	23%

This transition has significant consequences. For potential entrepreneurs, it's an opportunity to join existing businesses with loyal customers, functional systems, and income sources. It's an opportunity to avoid the exhausting startup phase and jump into a situation of power. For existing business owners, it's a chance to grow their businesses, explore new markets, and increase their efficiency through smart acquisitions.

But why is acquisition the optimal strategy in this scenario? First, it's about speed. In a world where markets evolve at breakneck speed, acquiring an existing business can be the quickest way to grow your footprint. Second, it's about risk mitigation. Established businesses come with a track record, financial history, and often a loyal customer base—all of which reduce the uncertainty that plagues new ventures. Third, it's about talent acquisition. Taking over a business also means inheriting a team with experience and industry knowledge, which can be invaluable.

To illustrate this point, let's look at an example of a successful acquisition that leveraged the benefits of buying a Baby Boomer-owned business. In 2019, Ms. J, the founder and CEO of a chain of artisanal bakeries in Houston, acquired The Pie Shop, a family-owned business that specialized in pies and cakes. The Pie Shop had been operating for over 40 years and was owned by Ms. B, who was looking to retire and sell her business.

The acquisition was a win-win situation for both parties. For Ms. J, it was an opportunity to expand her product line, access new customers, and tap into the expertise and reputation of The Pie Shop. She also retained most of the staff, who brought their skills and loyalty to the new venture. For Miss B, it was a chance to ensure the continuity and growth of her business, while receiving a fair price and a monthly income from seller financing. She also stayed on as a consultant for six months, helping with the transition and sharing her knowledge with Julia.

The result was a smooth integration and a thriving business. The Bakery increased its revenue by 25%, gained a loyal following of pie lovers, and strengthened its brand identity. The Pie Shop maintained its quality and service, while benefiting from The Bakery's marketing and operational systems. Ms. J and Ms. B also developed a strong relationship based on mutual respect and appreciation. By acquiring The Pie Shop, Ms. J not only grew her business but also honored and preserved Ms. B's legacy.

At the heart of this strategy is the need for a thoughtful approach. It's not about buying businesses indiscriminately but identifying those with synergy, potential for growth, and alignment with your vision. It requires due diligence, a clear understanding of valuation, and a solid integration plan.

Let's talk about financials. Acquiring a business often allows for creative financing solutions. Seller financing, for example, can alleviate the need for hefty upfront capital, making acquisitions more accessible. This is particularly relevant in deals with Baby Boomers, many of whom may prefer a steady income stream over a lump-sum payout as they ease into retirement.

Beyond the numbers, acquiring a Baby Boomer-owned business can also be a profound exercise in legacy preservation. Many of these entrepreneurs have poured their lives into their businesses, and the prospect of passing their life's work on to a capable successor who will honor and grow their legacy can be a compelling selling point. Of course, the path is not without its challenges. Cultural fit, customer retention, and the melding of different operational systems can all present hurdles in the post-acquisition phase. The key to overcoming these challenges is preparation and an unwavering commitment to open, transparent communication throughout the transition process.

What does this all mean for the future of small business in America? It signals a period of dynamic change, with fresh ideas and new energy revitalizing existing businesses. It represents a chance for economic growth, job creation, and innovation as new owners build on the foundations laid by their predecessors.

Motivations for Sale

The exodus of Boomers from the business landscape is reshaping the market as we know it. This generation, having ridden the wave of post-war prosperity to establish thriving enterprises, now stands at a crossroad. The decision to sell a business is monumental, and for many Boomers, it is a path chosen not just out of desire, but necessity. What drives these seasoned entrepreneurs to hand over the reins? Let's delve into the motivations behind their decisions.

A startling statistic unveils a critical gap in the business continuity of small enterprises: more than 58% of business owners lack a transition or succession plan. It's a figure that reflects both oversight and a complex relationship with the future. For a myriad of owners, building a business was a lifelong endeavor, but the blueprint did not extend to a clear handover. The absence of a plan is not merely an oversight; it's a silent alarm that signals the end of an era.

According to a survey by the International Business Brokers Association (IBBA), the top five reasons business owners sell are:

Top Reasons for Selling	Percentage of Sellers (Q2 2020)
Retirement	37%
Burnout	18%
Health Issues	12%
Family Issues	9%
New Opportunities	8%

- **Retirement:** This is the most common reason, accounting for 37% of sales in Q2 2020. Many Boomers are reaching the age where they want to enjoy their golden years and leave behind the stress of running a business.

- **Burnout:** Running a business can take a toll on one's physical and mental health, especially in times of crisis. 18% of sellers cited burnout as their primary motivation, indicating a need for a change of pace or lifestyle.

- **Health issues**: Unfortunately, some owners are forced to sell due to health problems that prevent them from managing their business effectively. This was the case for 12% of sellers in Q2 2020, highlighting the importance of having a contingency plan in place.

- **Family issues:** Another reason that may compel owners to sell is family issues, such as divorce, death, or relocation. These events can affect the owner's ability or willingness to continue operating the business. 9% of sellers reported this as their main reason for selling.

- **New opportunities:** Some owners may decide to sell because they have found or created new opportunities for themselves, such as pursuing a different career, starting a new venture, or investing in other businesses. 8% of sellers said this was their motivation for selling, demonstrating their entrepreneurial spirit and ambition.

Turning our gaze to the market, open listings reveal a landscape rich with opportunities. Each quarter, 30,000 to 40,000+ businesses are listed on the open market. This surge is not random—it's a demographic certainty. People are aging, and as they do, the market swells with businesses that carry the legacy of a generation. For new entrepreneurs, this is an open invitation to partake in the wealth of established businesses, rich in history and ripe for innovation.

The motivations for sale are not single-threaded. They weave through financial readiness, the pursuit of retirement, or the idea of new ventures. The economic impact of these sales is significant, with cash flow positive businesses changing hands, injecting fresh energy into the economy. It's a pivotal transfer of wealth from one generation to the next.

For owners, the decision to sell is often bittersweet. These businesses are not just assets; they are repositories of memories, hard work, and identity. Yet, the reality of age and change cannot be ignored. Selling becomes a process of letting go, of acknowledging that the time has come to pass the baton. It is an act of trust in the new generation, a belief that what was built will continue to flourish under new guardianship.

The Ripple Effect

Consider the statistics from the Small Business Administration, which estimates that approximately 10 million baby boomer-owned businesses will change hands between 2019 and 2029. This staggering figure represents a significant portion of the small business sector, with baby boomers owning about two-thirds of businesses with employees – that's around 4 million companies. As these entrepreneurs look toward retirement, the transfer of ownership through sales or acquisitions has the potential to reshape local economies and the national economic landscape.

This is important because small businesses are the core of the American economy. They make jobs, innovate, and compete. When a small business gets bought, it can cause many changes. The new owner can offer new ideas, invest in growth, and boost productivity. But it could also result in reshaping, cutting, or shutting down if the acquisition is handled badly.

The ripple effect starts with the employees. A change in ownership can be a time of uncertainty for staff, but it can also offer opportunities for career advancement, skill development, and increased wages. As employees' economic situations change, so too does their spending power, which can have a significant impact on local businesses and services.

One example of a successful generational wealth transfer through business acquisition is the story of Ben and Jerry's, the iconic ice cream brand. In 1978, Ben Cohen and Jerry Greenfield opened their first scoop shop in a renovated gas station in Vermont. They grew their business with a social mission, supporting local farmers, fair trade, and environmental causes. In 2000, they sold their company to Unilever, a multinational consumer goods giant, for $326 million.

But this was not a typical sell-out. Ben and Jerry's retained an independent board of directors, which had the final say over the brand's social and environmental policies, product quality, and marketing. Unilever agreed to respect the founders' values and vision, and to invest in the company's social impact initiatives. The deal also included a generous employee stock option plan, which allowed the workers to share in the profits.

The result was a win-win situation. Ben and Jerry's gained access to Unilever's global distribution network, research and development resources, and financial backing. Unilever benefited from the brand's loyal customer base, innovative flavors, and positive reputation. Both parties leveraged their strengths and learned from each other. Today, Ben and Jerry's is one of the most popular and profitable ice cream brands in the world, with annual sales of over $600 million. It also continues to be a leader in social and environmental activism, supporting causes such as racial justice, climate change, and democracy.

This example shows that generational wealth transfer through business acquisition can be more than just a monetary exchange. It can also be a way of preserving and enhancing the legacy of a business, while creating new opportunities for growth, innovation, and impact. It can be a collaboration between generations, rather than a competition. And it can be a catalyst for positive change in the world.

Furthermore, acquisition activity in the small business sector often leads to increased competition and better services. Acquisitions can enable companies to expand their offerings, improve customer service, and enter new markets. This not only benefits consumers but also forces competitors to step up their game, leading to a healthier market overall.

Beyond the immediate impact on employees and consumers, the effects of M&A can be seen in supplier networks and the broader business ecosystem. Small businesses are frequently interconnected through supply chains. When a small business grows following an acquisition, its suppliers often benefit from increased orders, leading to growth and job creation within those firms as well. Conversely, if an acquisition leads to the consolidation of suppliers, this could result in the loss of business for some and the potential for expansion for others.

An acquisition in small businesses also has tax effects. The buying or selling of a business can change taxes for the business owners and different levels of government. A well-handled acquisition can make it easier to transfer ownership, keeping up the businesses' economic support to public funds.

M&A activity triggers a need for a variety of professional services. Legal, financial, and consulting firms often see an uptick in business, creating jobs and income for those sectors. In turn, professionals in these industries may have more disposable income to spend, further stimulating the economy.

The ripple effects of successful acquisitions are not limited to the parties involved. They can have a positive impact on the entire economy, creating growth opportunities for other businesses and generating value for society. By pursuing strategic acquisitions, small businesses can become more competitive, resilient, and innovative, contributing to the overall health and dynamism of the market.

Chapter 3
GOOD, BETTER, BEST

A Look into the Average Investor Portfolio

The mine of business is full of treasures, but not all are equally shiny. Some are more valuable, more durable, and more rewarding than others. As an investor, you want to find the gems that will sparkle the most in your portfolio, the ones that will give you the best returns for your hard-earned money. But how do you distinguish the good from the better, and the better from the best? In this chapter, we will explore some of the most popular investment options available to you, and examine their pros and cons, their risks and rewards, and their suitability for your financial goals. We will compare and contrast three categories of investments. Each one has its own characteristics, advantages, and challenges, and each one can play a different role in your wealth-building journey. By the end, you will have a clearer idea of how to diversify your portfolio, based on your risk tolerance, time horizon, and personal preferences. Let's start digging into the mine and see what we can unearth.

Good: The Stock Market

Let's talk numbers, and nothing is more convincing than the historical data of the stock market. In particular, let's examine the S&P 500 index, a benchmark that reflects the U.S. economy through the performance of 500 large companies traded on stock exchanges in the United States. Over time, this index has yielded an average of 7-9% per year after accounting for inflation. This figure isn't just a number; it's a guide for what consistent, long-term investing can accomplish.

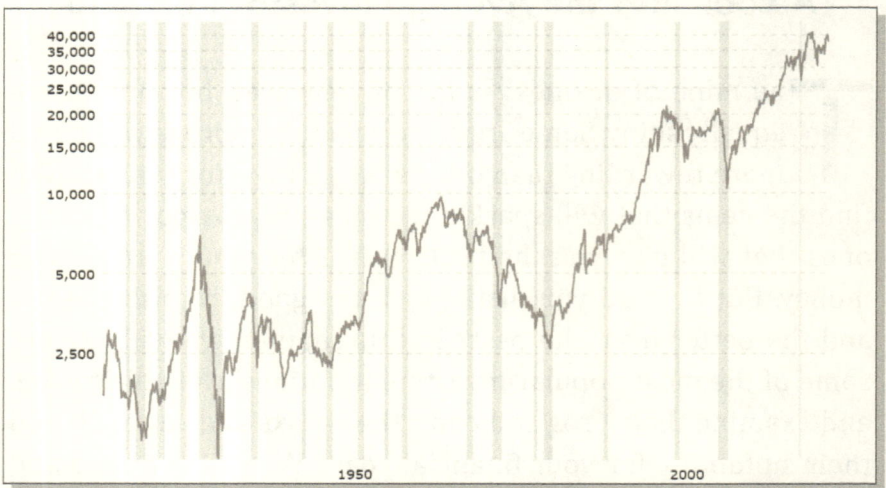

Dow Jones Industrial Average (DJIA) stock market index shows the last 100 years of data.

Consider this scenario: if you were to invest $10,000 annually with an average return of 8%, you wouldn't just have the sum of your contributions at the end of 20 years. Thanks to the power of compounding interest, where earnings are reinvested to generate their own earnings, your portfolio could grow to nearly $600,000 in that period. That's the magic of the stock market – the potential for money to grow much faster than it would in a typical savings account.

But the stock market isn't a get-rich-quick scheme. It's a tool for building wealth gradually over time. The key is a long-term, disciplined investing strategy. This means resisting the urge to pull out your investments when the market dips or trying to time the market for the perfect entry and exit points. It requires patience and an understanding that the market will experience ups and downs, but over time, it has historically trended upward. Or as Warren Buffett, one of the most successful investors of all time, famously said, "The stock market is a device for transferring money from the impatient to the patient."

Now, it's easy to look at the stock market as a roller coaster, with its peaks and valleys causing heart-racing excitement or stomach-dropping fear. However, a disciplined investor sees beyond the short-term volatility. They understand that each dip might be an opportunity to buy quality stocks at a discount, and every peak isn't necessarily a signal to sell but rather a testament to their investment strategy paying off.

This approach calls for a level of emotional detachment, where decisions are driven by research, analysis, and a solid financial plan rather than the highs and lows of market sentiments. It's about sticking to a predetermined strategy that might involve regular investments regardless of market conditions, also known as dollar-cost averaging. This technique helps to smooth out the volatility by spreading purchases over time, which can lead to buying more shares when prices are low and fewer shares when prices are high.

Furthermore, diversification plays a crucial role in mitigating risk. Rather than putting all your eggs in one basket, spreading investments across various sectors, geographies, and asset classes can protect your portfolio from the downfall of any single investment. It's the equivalent of having multiple pathways to reach your financial goals; if one path encounters a roadblock, the others can pick up the slack.

To navigate the stock market successfully, it's also critical to stay informed. This doesn't mean you need to watch the ticker tape every second or become a financial analyst, but having a basic understanding of economic indicators, company performance metrics, and market trends can help you make more informed decisions. The knowledge will empower you to have confident conversations with financial advisors, understand the potential impact of world events on your investments and stay aligned with your long-term financial vision.

Better: Real Estate

At the heart of its appeal is the historical consistency of real estate appreciation. While stocks can skyrocket or plummet in the blink of an eye, real estate follows a steadier trajectory. On average, property values have ascended at a rate of 3-5% annually, though this figure can dance higher or dip lower based on the whims of location and market conditions. Yet even with these variances, the trendline of real estate value points unwaveringly upwards over the long term, painting a picture of enduring stability and growth.

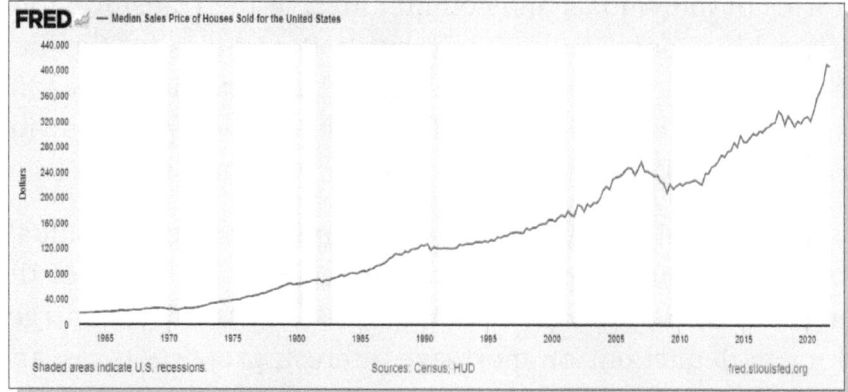

The benefits of investing in real estate are multifaceted. First, there's the allure of rental income—a steady stream of cash flow that fills an investor's coffers every month. This passive income can serve as a cushion during economic downturns or a supplement to other earnings, offering a financial buoyancy that is hard to replicate with other investments.

Then there's the appreciation of property value, a slow and steady race won by the tortoises of the investment world. This appreciation is not merely a hope of speculation; it is a well-documented historical trend backed by a finite supply of land and the ever-growing demand for space to live, work, and play.

But perhaps the most grounding benefit of real estate investment is the tangible asset security it offers. Real estate is a physical asset, one that cannot vanish into thin air like a bad stock investment or a bankrupt company. It's there, under your feet, a patch of the Earth that has intrinsic value simply by virtue of its existence. It's a piece of the planet, and as Mark Twain famously quipped, "Buy land, they're not making it anymore."

Yet, the true essence of real estate investment is not captured by statistics, cash flows, or tangible assets alone. It is found in the stories of individuals and communities, in the transformation of neighborhoods, and in the security it provides for families. It's about the pride of ownership and the creation of lasting legacies. It's about the peace of mind that comes from knowing you have a solid asset that can weather economic storms.

In practical terms, real estate investment enables individuals to leverage their capital, borrowing against the value of the property to multiply potential gains. It offers tax advantages through deductions on mortgage interest, property taxes, and depreciation. It allows for a hands-on approach to increasing value through improvements and management or a hands-off approach through real estate investment trusts (REITs) and other passive investment opportunities.

To navigate the real estate investment landscape with poise, one must understand the local market, zoning laws, and the economic factors that drive demand. It requires due diligence, a keen eye for potential, and, often, a willingness to roll up one's sleeves. It's not just about buying a property; it's about cultivating it, nurturing it, and ultimately watching it grow.

The path to wealth through real estate is not a sprint; it's a marathon. It's about building a portfolio brick by brick, property by property, with each acquisition a testament to the investor's acumen and vision. It's a journey that can transform not just individual fortunes but also revitalize communities and reshape cities.

Best: Business Acquisition

Acquisition is like striking gold in a mine. You never know how much you will find until you dig deeper. Unlike passive investments such as stocks and real estate, which typically offer single-digit percentage returns, acquisition can unearth a treasure trove of value. Imagine the possibility of securing a 20%, 50%, or even a staggering 100% return in the first-year post-acquisition. This isn't mere speculation; it's a reality for those who strategically navigate the acquisition landscape.

Acquisition presents an active investment choice, one that demands involvement and a keen understanding of the market. It's about identifying synergies where one plus one equals three. When done correctly, it can yield immediate value uplift and set the stage for sustained growth over time. This growth is not just in terms of financial returns but also in market positioning, operational efficiency, and strategic advantage.

Comparatively, traditional investment avenues like stocks and real estate can seem less dynamic. Stocks, for instance, are subject to the whims of the market. Real estate investments, while tangible, can be laden with management challenges and market saturation. Acquisition, on the other hand, thrives on the principle of control. Investors who acquire take an active role in shaping the destiny of their investments. They're not just betting on market conditions; they are creating value through strategic maneuvers and operational enhancements.

While stocks and real estate may seem like safe investments, they also come with a price: liquidity. When you invest in these passive assets, you have to put your money to sleep and hope for the best. You're at the mercy of market fluctuations, regulatory changes, and other external factors. You can't access your money easily, and if you do, you may lose out on potential gains or incur penalties.

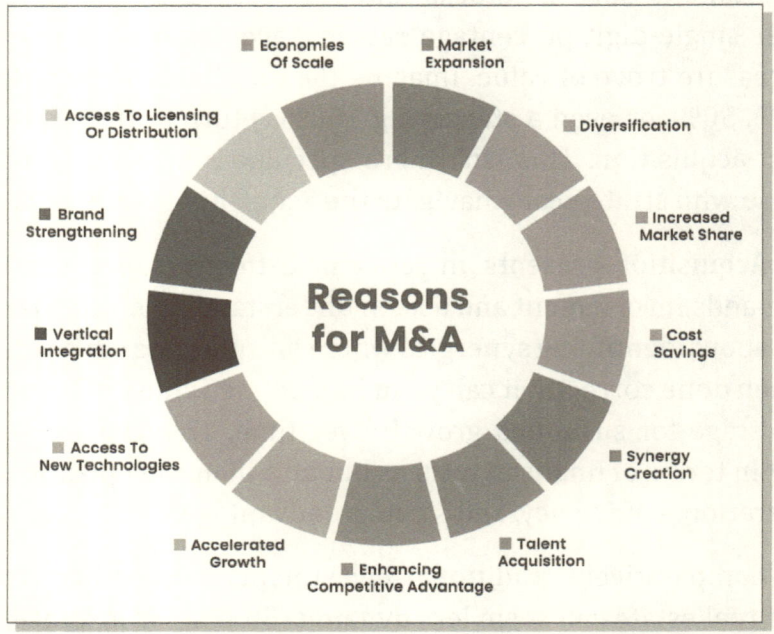

Acquisition, on the other hand, comes with instant cash flow. You're not just buying an asset; you're buying a revenue stream. You're acquiring customers, contracts, intellectual property, and talent. You're tapping into a source of value that can generate returns from day one. You're not waiting for your money to wake up; you're waking it up stronger.

But how does one strike gold in this minefield of opportunity? It begins with a thorough understanding of the acquisition process – from scouting potential targets to due diligence, negotiation, integration, and beyond. It's about recognizing not just the financial metrics but also the cultural fit between companies, the potential for growth, and the pathways to unlock hidden value.

Perhaps the most captivating element of a deal is the treasure it uncovers. These are stories of alchemy where the merged entities often achieve what neither could have in isolation. It's where the whole is indeed more than its parts and where the right leadership can guide this newly forged entity toward undiscovered realms of success.

Of course, with greater potential comes greater risk. Business acquisition is not a silver bullet, and not all acquisitions lead to success stories. The path is fraught with challenges and pitfalls, from overvaluation and cultural mismatches to integration issues and customer retention concerns. However, for those equipped with the right knowledge, advisors, and timing, the rewards can far outweigh the risks.

Thus, Mergers & Acquisitions should not be viewed as an exclusive playground for the corporate giants. Middle-market companies and even smaller enterprises can leverage this tactic to leapfrog their competition and achieve exponential growth. It's about being bold, about recognizing the transformative power of takeover, and about seizing the opportunity to turn the tide in your favor.

The crux of the matter is that business acquisition is not just about financial engineering; it's about strategic vision. It's for those who look beyond the immediate horizon, those who envision a future where they have reshaped their business landscape. It's a journey of calculated risks and strategic planning, with the potential for returns that can redefine an investor's portfolio.

So, are you ready to take the plunge and join the ranks of successful business acquirers? Are you ready to transform your financial future and create lasting value for yourself and your stakeholders? You need to be smart, savvy, and prepared. M&A is not a game of chance; it's a game of skill. It's not about finding a needle in a haystack; it's about mining for gold. And it's not about settling for good or better; it's about striving for the best. That's why we have written this book: to help you master the art and science of M&A, and to guide you through the process from start to finish.

Chapter 4
ENTREPRENEURSHIP IS HARD

One of the most enduring myths of entrepreneurship is that starting a business from scratch is the only way to strike gold. The image of the lone miner, digging his own tunnel, chipping away at the rocks, and hoping to uncover a vein of precious metal is a powerful one. It appeals to our sense of adventure, creativity, and independence. But it also obscures a more practical and profitable alternative: buying an existing mine that already has proven reserves, equipment, and workers. This way, the entrepreneur can bypass the risks and challenges of building something from zero, and instead focus on optimizing and expanding the business. This is the essence of acquisition, a strategy that can offer a faster and safer route to the entrepreneurial dream.

The Alluring Illusion

Dreams of exploration are the pulsing heart of the entrepreneurial spirit. The ability to discover new resources, to dig deeper than others, and to unearth hidden treasures is an intoxicating possibility. It's the pickaxe in the hand of the miner, the uncharted cavern awaiting the first strike. Entrepreneurs are adventurers who seek beyond the surface, finding opportunities, markets, and solutions that have yet to be exploited. For them, the thrill of discovery is a reward, a testament to the human capacity for curiosity and courage.

Tied closely to that, creative freedom is the financial reward. The narrative of entrepreneurship is rich with tales of self-made success, of individuals who have turned ideas into fortunes. There's a magnetic pull to these stories, a gravitational force that attracts those who yearn to be the architects of their own financial futures. The potential of a business to scale, to generate wealth that transcends generations, is a compelling force for many who choose this path.

Beyond the personal gains, there's a yearning to leave a lasting impact. Entrepreneurs often nurture a vision of contributing to the world in a meaningful way, whether it's through innovative products that change how we live, philanthropic endeavors that address societal needs, or by setting new standards in ethical business practices. The legacy of a business can ripple through time, touching lives and shaping the future long after its founder has stepped away.

Yet, the journey of entrepreneurship is not a smooth, well-lit road. It is riddled with obstacles that cast dark shadows, testing the grit and ingenuity of even the most resolute explorers. The stark truth is that the entrepreneurial terrain is strewn with the wreckage of ventures that have stumbled and fallen. Every strike of the pickaxe is accompanied by the risk of hitting a dead end, the possibility of exhausting one's resources, and the daunting prospect of digging a new tunnel.

These challenges are manifold and merciless. Market dynamics can shift like quicksand underfoot, competitors emerge with alarming speed, and the very innovation that fuels a business can be rendered obsolete by the relentless march of technology.

In confronting these challenges, the entrepreneur learns that resilience is not just a trait but a craft honed through experience and the will to persevere. It is the skill that is acquired by mining through the rocks of disappointment and uncertainty, and it is the shield that guards the dream against the blasts and explosions of an often ruthless marketplace.

Cash Flow Matters

Startups and new businesses face the difficult problem of negative cash flow. In the beginning stages, companies are at risk as they try to find their market position, often spending more than they earn to support growth and build their brand. This financial balancing act is shown by the harsh business survival rates: about 20% of businesses fail in the first year. While two-thirds may reach their second anniversary, only about a third will have the endurance to pass the ten-year mark.

Negative cash flow can arise from various sources, such as high upfront costs, overinvestment in inventory, slow-paying customers, or simply overestimating market demand. This financial conundrum requires entrepreneurs to have a keen eye on their cash positions at all times, ensuring they have the necessary funds to cover their immediate and future obligations.

The consequences of negative cash flow can be dire. It restricts a company's ability to invest in new opportunities, pay for essential services, or even meet payroll. This can lead to a vicious cycle: as suppliers and employees lose confidence, the business may face higher costs and decreased productivity, further exacerbating the cash flow problem.

However, there is light at the end of the tunnel. Entrepreneurs who dig their way out of this predicament often come out stronger, with a more solid business model and a better grasp of their financial terrain. They learn to manage their cash flow by keeping an eye on it at all times, trimming down excess costs, and finding creative ways to boost revenue or secure funding.

To escape the cash flow cave-in, business owners must drill down and be alert. This involves prudent forecasting, creating a cash buffer, and arranging credit lines before they are needed. Additionally, enhancing the accounts receivable process can keep the cash flowing; this might include offering rewards for early payments or applying more rigorous credit standards.

Business owners who can master these skills will not only survive but thrive in the competitive and dynamic market. They will be able to adapt to changing customer demands, seize new opportunities, and overcome any challenges that may arise along the way. By doing so, they will avoid joining the ranks of failed businesses and instead carve out their own success stories.

Pitfalls of Business

Business failure is a ruthless and relentless reality. Companies face constant challenges from shifts and preferences in the market. A single mistake, a single neglect, and a business can be relegated to the history of those who did not survive.

For new entrepreneurs, the terrain is particularly treacherous. They often face additional barriers, such as limited access to capital, fewer networking opportunities, and systemic biases that can stifle growth before it even begins. The statistics paint a picture of disparity, but within this challenge lies an opportunity—an opportunity for business owners to create, disrupt, and claim their rightful place in the market.

Businesses that can pivot in response to changing market conditions, that can identify and exploit niches, and that can turn potential threats into opportunities are the ones that will not only survive but thrive. For small businesses, this means embracing the unique perspectives and experiences they bring to the table, which can become their greatest assets in distinguishing themselves from the competition.

In the face of adversity, these businesses must forge alliances, seek out mentors, and build robust networks that can provide support and open doors to new possibilities. They need to be relentless in their pursuit of knowledge and understanding of the market, their customers, and the ever-evolving landscape of technology that can give them an edge.

The mine is not forgiving; it does not spare anyone. It tests every miner, but the burden on small miners is heavier. Therefore, it is crucial for these miners to leverage their collective power, seek out resources designed to help them, and advocate for policies that protect their rights.

Innovative strategies like mergers and acquisitions (M&A) can be particularly potent for businesses looking to scale quickly and establish a significant market presence. An acquisition strategy allows businesses to gain new capabilities, access to new markets, and the opportunity to diversify their revenue streams. For Main Street businesses, this can be a game-changer—a way to leapfrog the barriers and establish themselves as formidable players in the market.

Chapter 5
SUITABILITY

Not all acquisitions are created equal. Some may fail to deliver the expected benefits or even destroy value for investors. Success depends on various factors, such as the strategic fit, the valuation, the integration process, and the market conditions. Therefore, it is crucial to assess the suitability of a transaction before investing in it. Suitability refers to how well a deal aligns with your investment goals, risk appetite, time horizon, and portfolio composition.

Just as gold miners need to sift through tons of dirt to find the precious metal, investors need to evaluate numerous deal opportunities to find the ones that suit their needs. Not every shiny object is gold, and not every acquisition is a good fit for your portfolio. Suitability is the key to ensuring that you invest in deals that match your profile and expectations and avoid those that don't. By doing so, you can enhance your portfolio's performance and diversify your sources of income.

Aspiring Entrepreneurs

Consider the value proposition of acquisition: it provides an opportunity to acquire an existing business with a proven track record, a customer base, established operations, and cash flow from day one. This is a stark contrast to starting a business from scratch, which often involves a steep learning curve, the challenge of building a customer base, and a period without income.

Furthermore, an acquisition approach can mitigate the risks associated with entrepreneurship. A new venture is inherently risky, with many unknown variables. In contrast, acquiring an established business allows you to analyze historical data, assess the company's financial health, and make an informed decision.

The financial aspect of an acquisition should not be overlooked. While buying a business requires capital, there are various financing options available. Seller financing, traditional bank loans, and Small Business Administration (SBA) loans are potential resources. Investing in a business with a strong cash flow can provide immediate financial returns, and the business itself is an asset that can appreciate in value over time.

According to a survey by Guidant Financial, the most common reason people start their own businesses is to be their own boss, followed by pursuing their passion and having a better work-life balance. The table below shows the distribution of reasons people start businesses, based on 3,100 respondents.

Reasons people start businesses	Percentage
Be their own Boss	60%
Corporate life dissatisfaction	47%
Passion	31%
Opportunity	21%
Unemployment	23%
Not ready to retire	23%

Data Source: Forbes Advisor

The pie chart also reveals the average amount of money that people invest in starting their own businesses from scratch. The largest segment of respondents, 27.3%, invested between $250,000 and $500,000 in their ventures, followed by 17.6% who invested less than $5,000. The chart indicates that starting a business from scratch can require a significant amount of capital, depending on the type and scale of the business.

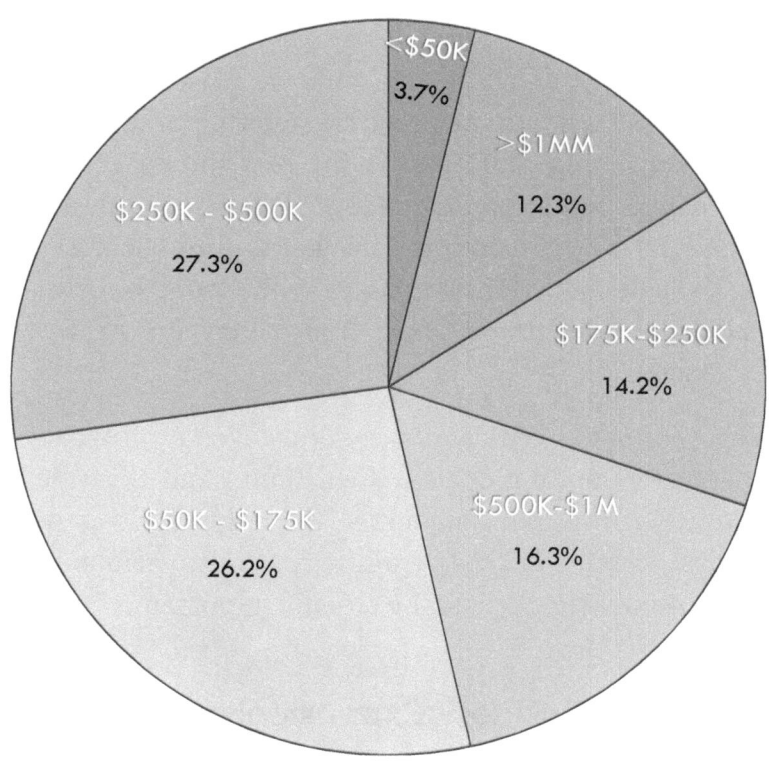

Data Source: Forbes Advisor

One of the most compelling reasons for choosing M&A as your pathway to entrepreneurship is the opportunity for mentorship. Often, the seller is invested in the success of the business post-sale and may provide invaluable guidance during the transition period. This mentorship can be a game-changer, offering insights into the business's operations, customer relationships, and industry dynamics.

M&A also allows you to leverage your previous experience in new ways. The skills you've honed in your current profession – be it leadership, strategic thinki.ng, or operations management – can be directly applied to running a business. Your unique perspective can bring fresh ideas to the table, driving innovation and competitive advantage.

Now, let's talk about the practical steps to pursue a takeover. Start by identifying your areas of interest and expertise. What industries are you passionate about? Where can you leverage your skills? Then, research the market to find businesses that are up for sale. Look for companies with strong fundamentals but also consider those that offer room for growth and improvement.

Negotiation is a critical phase in takeover. Approach it with a clear understanding of your own limits and the value you place on the business. Remember, the negotiation is not just about price; terms such as training periods, various clauses, and transitional support can be equally important.

Business Expansionists

Acquiring additional businesses is not just a matter of adding new products or services to your portfolio; it's a transformative strategy that can catapult your business to new heights. When you merge with or acquire another company, you're not solely gaining their customer base or their product lines—you're also absorbing their market knowledge, their operational efficiencies, and potentially, their innovative culture. This can lead to synergies that are not possible through organic growth alone. Consider the multiplied impact. By acquiring a business, you can double your customer base overnight. If the acquired company is in a related field, you can cross-sell products to a wider audience and quickly scale operations. Moreover, if they possess unique technologies or processes, you can integrate these to create a competitive edge that would take years to develop internally.

But it's not just about the numbers; it's about strategic positioning. Through takeover, you have the opportunity to enter new markets more swiftly and assertively. This could mean geographical expansion or diversifying into new industry sectors, which organically would require considerable time and resources.

The financial aspect of acquisition cannot be overlooked either. Acquiring a profitable business can provide immediate cash flow and earnings growth. It can also lead to cost synergies—by consolidating overheads and streamlining operations, profitability can be enhanced. Additionally, there's the potential to access new capital, whether through the acquired company's existing financing arrangements or by leveraging the combined entity's increased assets.

The process requires a thorough evaluation of potential targets, a clear understanding of how the acquisition aligns with your business goals, and careful planning to integrate the new company into your existing operations. The risks include cultural clashes, overestimation of synergies, and the challenge of managing a larger organization.

Yet, with these risks come tremendous rewards. Successful takeovers have been known to redefine industries, turning modest-sized businesses into market leaders. They can also act as a catalyst for further growth, setting a precedent for continuous expansion through strategic acquisitions.

Corporate Executives

An executive who is moving to business acquisition is stepping into a fresh and thrilling domain of entrepreneurship, where they can leverage their expertise and knowledge in leadership, strategy, and management to generate value and influence. Business acquisition is a type of entrepreneurship that involves acquiring and expanding an established business, rather than building one from the ground up.

These professionals have leadership skills that are valuable for entrepreneurship. They can lead teams, projects, and initiatives, and influence different stakeholders, like customers, employees, investors, and regulators. These skills can help them run and grow a business they acquire, as they can share a clear vision, encourage and inspire others, and make strong relationships and partnerships. Leadership skills help entrepreneurs cope with the unpredictability and complexity of their work and manage the mental and emotional difficulties they face.

These leaders know how to organize and manage a business in terms of its legal, financial, and operational aspects. They also know how to navigate the regulatory and compliance issues that affect the industry and the market. These skills are valuable for buying private companies, as they can help the executive to evaluate the target company's strengths and weaknesses, identify and mitigate any risks or liabilities, and ensure a smooth and efficient integration process. Understanding corporate structure and governance also helps the executive to communicate and negotiate effectively with the sellers, the lenders, and the advisors involved in the acquisition. By leveraging their knowledge and experience in this area, the executive can increase the likelihood of a successful outcome.

Strategy is another skill that they possess that can help them in the acquisition space. Executives are good at creating and carrying out strategic plans, goals, and objectives, and making sure they are consistent with the mission and vision of the organization. These are essential skills for finding and assessing potential acquisition targets, and for developing and applying a value proposition that sets the acquired business apart from its competitors. Strategy skills also enable the executive to track and evaluate the performance and progress of the acquisition, and to change and adapt as needed.

Executives have experience in scaling and optimizing a business, such as increasing production, expanding operations, enhancing quality, and lowering costs. They also know how to identify and pursue new opportunities, such as exploring new territories, extracting new resources, or acquiring new equipment. These are essential skills for finding and evaluating potential acquisition targets, and for integrating and improving the acquired business.

A professional who is transitioning to business acquisition can leverage their skills and experience to succeed and thrive in the entrepreneurial space. By learning new skills and knowledge, such as valuation, due diligence, negotiation, and innovation, the executive can enhance their entrepreneurial capabilities and potential. Business acquisition can be a rewarding and fulfilling career option for an executive who is looking for a new challenge and a new opportunity.

Structured Transitioners

The discipline that professional athletes and military personnel develop is unparalleled. It's the kind of rigorous self-control and commitment to a regimen that ensures peak performance under the most challenging circumstances. In the acquisition space, this discipline translates into the meticulous analysis of potential acquisition targets, the patience required in due diligence, and the steadfast adherence to a strategic vision. Just as a disciplined training schedule leads to athletic success, a disciplined approach to M&A can lead to successful business growth and expansion.

Leadership is another transferable trait that is central to both arenas. In sports and the military, leadership doesn't just mean being at the front of the pack or giving orders; it's about inspiring others, making strategic decisions, and being accountable for the outcomes. In business, especially during the complex processes of takeover, effective leadership involves guiding a team through evaluations, negotiations, and the intricacies of integrating different corporate cultures post-acquisition. The ability to lead with vision and integrity is crucial to navigating the often rocky terrain of a takeover.

Teamwork is the third pillar that stands firm in both the competitive sports and military environments and is equally important in business. In takeover, no deal is the effort of a single person; it requires a team of skilled individuals from financial advisors to legal experts. The camaraderie and ability to work cohesively towards a common goal, so essential on the playing field or in a military operation, are just as vital when orchestrating a successful business merger or acquisition.

Now, you might wonder, how does one channel these skills into a successful acquisition strategy? First and foremost, it's about recognizing the value of your honed attributes and how they apply to business. Take the discipline; it's about setting clear goals for what you want your business acquisition to achieve and systematically working towards them. As in sports or military training, there's a need for consistent effort and a focus on the end game.

Leadership in acquisition means being the driving force behind your business vision. It's about scouting for companies that align with your goals and steering negotiations in a way that benefits all parties. Just as a captain leads a team to victory, your leadership can turn a potential deal into a thriving business venture.

And let's not forget teamwork. Completing a successful acquisition is a collaborative effort. It requires a network of professionals who can bring different strengths to the table. You need to build a team that trusts each other's expertise, much like a military unit relies on the unique skills of its members to complete a mission.

In addition to these core skills, understanding the financial landscape is key. Athletes and military personnel are no strangers to strategy and planning, and these skills are directly transferable to financial planning and assessment in the acquisition process. Learning to assess the financial health of a potential acquisition and understanding the market in which it operates is akin to studying the playbook of an opponent or strategizing a military campaign.

Moreover, the ability to adapt and overcome adversity, a trait well-developed in the high-pressure environments of professional sports and military service, is invaluable in the M&A world. Deals can change rapidly, unexpected challenges can arise, and the ability to pivot and craft creative solutions is often the difference between success and failure.

Portfolio Builders

Acquisition is a powerful tool for mining value from the market. Just as miners extract precious metals from the earth, investors can unearth hidden gems by acquiring or merging with other companies. M&A can create value in various ways, such as lowering costs, increasing revenues, diversifying risks, and sparking innovation. These benefits can translate into higher returns and a stronger portfolio for the investor.

When a company acquires or merges with another, it can unlock value in several ways. Economies of scale are achieved as larger organizations benefit from lower costs per unit due to increased production. There's also the potential for revenue synergies, where the combined company can cross-sell products to new customer bases or enter markets that were previously out of reach. This can lead to increased sales and, consequently, a boost in the investment's value.

Diversification is another key advantage of a takeover. By acquiring companies in different industries or geographic locations, an investor can spread risk across various markets.

This helps insulate the portfolio from sector-specific downturns or regional economic slumps. Consider an investor whose portfolio is heavily concentrated in the technology sector; by acquiring a well-established manufacturing company, they can reduce their exposure to the volatility of the tech industry.

Furthermore, M&A can be a gateway to innovation. Companies often acquire to harness the innovative products or services of smaller, agile firms. This can lead to a significant competitive edge and, by extension, increase the value of the investment. For instance, a traditional retail company acquiring a cutting-edge e-commerce platform can transform its business model to thrive in the digital age.

Tax advantages are also a consideration. The structuring of deals can lead to tax benefits that can improve the bottom line of the combined entity. These savings can then be passed on to investors in the form of higher returns.

However, it's crucial to approach acquisition with a strategic mindset. Due diligence is imperative to understanding the intrinsic value of the target company and to evaluate how well it complements the acquiring firm's business model. Poorly executed acquisitions can lead to a mismatch in corporate cultures, redundant technologies, or a dilution of the brand, which could erode investment value rather than enhance it.

Investors should also be aware of the timing of their deal activities. Market conditions fluctuate, and acquiring during a downturn might allow for more favorable terms, while buying at the peak could result in overpayment for the target company. It is about striking the right balance and seizing opportunities when they present themselves.

A deal should not be a reckless dig for gold or a rush for quick profits. It requires a long-term vision, as the true value of an acquisition often emerges over time. Patience is key, as is the willingness to endure the initial mining phase, which can be rocky.

Chapter 6
FUNDABILITY

Acquiring another company is not just a matter of finding the right target and striking a deal. It also requires securing the funds to make it happen. How you finance your acquisition can have a significant impact on your return on investment, your risk exposure, and your future growth prospects. In this chapter, we will explore the different options available to finance your acquisition, from debt to equity to hybrid instruments. We will also discuss the pros and cons of each option, and how to choose the best one for your situation. Whether you are a seasoned acquirer or a novice in the field, you need to know your fundability – how to access and leverage the capital you need to make your acquisition a success.

Acquiring another company is not just a matter of finding the right vein and striking gold. It also requires securing the resources to make it happen. How you finance your acquisition can have a significant impact on your return on investment, your risk exposure, and your future growth prospects. In this chapter, we will explore the different tools available to finance your acquisition, from loans to shares to hybrid instruments. We will also discuss the pros and cons of each tool, and how to choose the best one for your situation. Whether you are a seasoned miner or a novice in the field, you need to know your fundability – how to access and leverage the resources you need to make your acquisition a success.

Eligibility

Imagine a world where businesses expand not only naturally but by buying other companies. This is not just for the big corporations; smaller ones can also do this. But before jumping in, let's simplify the difficulties and show what you need to be a player in this financial game.

At the heart of eligibility lies your financial health. Lenders aren't just handing out funds; they're investing in your potential to grow and repay. Your balance sheets, cash flow statements, and income statements become your resume. They must show profitability, liquidity, and a solid track record of financial performance. It's like proving your worth in a high-stakes interview – your past and present financials speak volumes about your future capabilities.

Beyond the numbers, your strategic positioning is key. Do you have a clear understanding of the industry you're looking to enter or expand within through acquisition? Your market insight and business plan need to demonstrate not just viability but also how the acquisition will propel your growth. It's not enough to have a target in mind; you must articulate how this move fits into the larger puzzle of your business strategy.

Creditworthiness is another cornerstone of eligibility. Like a beacon signaling to lenders, your credit score and history can either open doors or close them. It's akin to a trust score – a low credit score might signal risk, while a high score can pave the way for better financing terms. But it's not just about the score;

it's the history behind it that tells a story of reliability and fiscal responsibility.

Having the right team also factors into eligibility. Do you have advisors, accountants, and legal counsel who not only understand the intricacies of acquisition financing but are also adept at navigating its challenges? They're your strategists and tacticians, ensuring that due diligence is thorough and the transaction is structured to your advantage. It's not a solo journey; it's a coordinated effort requiring expertise and experience.

Your capital structure plays a role. How much equity are you bringing to the table? Lenders want to see skin in the game – a sign of commitment and confidence in your own venture. Your contribution can't be a token gesture; it needs to be substantial enough to align your interests with those of the lender.

We should also remember the significance of a well-defined exit strategy. Lenders need confidence that there's a realistic way to conclude the financing agreement positively, whether it's by selling, refinancing, or another means. It's like having a clear goal before you start the journey.

And what about the target company itself? It needs to be assessed for synergies, compatibility, and the potential for value creation. The perfect acquisition target isn't just about financial metrics; it's about how it complements and enhances your existing operations.

But there's more to it than ticking boxes on a checklist. Eligibility is also about timing and context. Is the market favorable? Are there geopolitical or economic factors that could affect the success of the acquisition? It's not just about being ready; it's about whether it's the right time to make a move.

Navigating Lending

SBA Loans

Small Business Administration (SBA) loans emerge as a beacon of hope for many entrepreneurs. These loans are designed to assist small businesses in getting off the ground and are equally valuable when acquiring an existing business. The SBA doesn't lend money directly but guarantees loans provided by participating lenders, typically requiring at least a 10% down payment.

The appeal of an SBA loan lies in its relatively lower down payment and more flexible terms compared to conventional loans. It's a viable option for those who might not have the hefty collateral often demanded by traditional lending avenues. But it's not without its challenges; the process can be daunting, with stringent documentation and eligibility requirements.

Conventional Loans

Moving on to conventional loans, these are the stalwarts of the lending world. Offered by banks and financial institutions, they don't carry the backing of a government agency. They often mandate a more substantial down payment, usually around 20% or more.

The stringent nature of conventional loans is a double-edged sword. On one side, they offer the simplicity of a more straightforward lending process without the red tape associated with government-guaranteed loans. On the other, they demand a more robust financial position from the borrower, potentially excluding those without significant capital from their ranks.

Unlimited SBA Loan Financing

Now, the concept of unlimited SBA loan financing might sound like an entrepreneur's utopia. However, it's crucial to understand what this truly entails. There isn't an infinite pool of money to dip into; rather, there are SBA programs that allow for significant loan amounts subject to the borrower meeting specific criteria.

The SBA 7(a) program, for example, can be a powerful tool in the acquisition arsenal, with loan amounts that can soar up to $5 million. This can be a game-changer for businesses that qualify, offering a level of financial support that could turn an ambitious acquisition into a tangible success.

Each of these lending options carries its own set of pros and cons, and the path you choose will be as unique as your business. As with any financial decision, it's critical to conduct thorough due diligence, consult with financial advisors, and consider the immediate and long-term implications of the loan you take on.

Seller Finance

Another option for financing your business acquisition is seller financing, where the seller agrees to lend you a portion of the purchase price. This can be a flexible and convenient way to supplement your own savings or traditional loans, as it reduces the amount of money you need upfront and shows the lender that the seller has confidence in the business. Seller financing can also help you negotiate better terms and interest rates, as the seller has a vested interest in your success.

Seller financing typically ranges from 10% to 60% of the purchase price, depending on the size and profitability of the business, the seller's motivation, and the buyer's creditworthiness. The repayment period can vary from a few years to a decade or more, and the interest rate can be fixed or variable, depending on the agreement. Some sellers may require collateral or a personal guarantee from the buyer, while others may accept a share of the future profits or equity as security.

Seller financing can be an attractive option for buyers who want to minimize their risk and leverage their cash flow, as well as for sellers who want to expedite the sale and defer taxes on their income. However, it also comes with some drawbacks, such as the possibility of default, dispute, or fraud. Therefore, it's vital to conduct due diligence, verify the financial statements and projections of the business, and consult with legal and financial advisors before entering into a seller financing agreement.

Financing Options

One of the advantages of financing your business acquisition is that there is no limit to the number of transactions you can do, as long as you have the funds and the opportunities. Unlike real estate, where you may face restrictions on the number of properties you can own or mortgages you can take, business acquisition allows you to diversify your portfolio and scale your income without any legal barriers.

When you are looking for financing options for your acquisition, you need to be aware of the lending criteria that different sources may have. For example, banks and credit unions may have stricter requirements on the loan-to-value ratio, the debt service coverage ratio, the credit score, and the collateral of the borrower. They may also limit the types of transactions they are willing to finance, such as asset-based or cash-flow-based deals. On the other hand, alternative lenders, such as online platforms, private equity firms, or angel investors, may offer more flexibility and creativity in structuring the financing, but they may also charge higher interest rates, fees, or equity stakes. It's essential to compare and contrast the pros and cons of each financing source and find the one that best suits your needs and goals.

Therefore, it's important to have a clear vision and criteria for what kind of businesses you want to acquire, how much you are willing to spend, and how you will finance them. By doing so, you can make smart and informed decisions that will maximize your profits and minimize your risks. Remember, quality over quantity is the key to success in business acquisition.

Utilizing Savings

Personal savings can serve as a solid foundation for financing your business acquisition. By allocating a portion of your savings towards the down payment, you not only demonstrate commitment to potential lenders and investors but also retain a degree of control over the financial structure of your acquisition. It's crucial to assess how much of your savings should go towards this purpose. Consider your personal financial security, the needs of dependents, and the existence of an emergency fund. It's about striking a balance – investing enough to make the acquisition feasible without jeopardizing your financial well-being.

Beyond the down payment, there are other acquisition-related expenses to consider. Due diligence, legal fees, and potential renovation costs are just a few examples. These expenses can accumulate quickly, and it's essential to account for them when determining how much of your savings to commit.

An overly optimistic approach could leave you financially exposed if unexpected costs arise.

When utilizing personal savings, the mindset should be one of strategic investment rather than mere spending. You're not just buying a business; you're investing in an asset that has the potential to generate cash flow and grow in value. This requires a diligent analysis of the business's financial statements, market position, and growth potential. It's critical to understand the business's cash flow patterns, as this will influence how quickly and reliably you can expect a return on your investment.

However, caution is key. Investing personal savings into a business acquisition is inherently risky. The future is unpredictable, and external factors such as market shifts or economic downturns can impact the performance of your new venture. Therefore, it's advisable to have a risk management plan in place. This could include insurance policies, diversification of your investment portfolio, and a solid exit strategy should the need arise.

Leveraging Equity

Think of your personal equity as a gold mine, one you've been digging into, perhaps unknowingly, with every paycheck, every investment, and every financial decision you've made up to this point. The beauty of this gold mine is its richness and the potential it holds to propel you into the realm of business ownership.

Take, for instance, your retirement funds. While traditionally viewed as a nest egg for the golden years, under certain circumstances, these funds can be repurposed to invest in your acquisition. Programs like Rollovers as Business Start-Ups (ROBS) allow you to tap into your retirement savings without incurring early withdrawal penalties or taxes. This approach isn't free from risk, and it certainly isn't for everyone, but for the right individual, it can be a game-changer.

Then there are your stocks and other investments. These can be liquidated, or you might consider taking a loan against your portfolio. Known as securities-based lending, this strategy lets you borrow against the value of your stocks without selling them. This keeps you invested in the market while providing the liquidity you need. Again, it's crucial to consider the potential risks, like the possibility of a margin call if the market dips and the value of your securities decreases.

But it's not just about what's in your portfolio; it's also about leveraging the equity in your home. A home equity line of credit (HELOC) can be a relatively low-interest way to access cash. You're borrowing against the value of your house, which can be a substantial amount if you've built up significant equity. This can be particularly attractive because of the potential tax benefits and the typically lower interest rates compared to other forms of lending.

Beyond these more traditional sources, you may also explore tapping into the value of other personal assets, such as life insurance policies with a cash value component, valuable collectibles, or even the equity in your vintage car. Each asset class comes with its unique set of considerations, but the underlying principle remains the same: your assets can be more than just a safety net; they can be the springboard into business ownership.

The key to effectively leveraging your equity is in the strategic, judicious application of these resources. It's not about putting all your eggs in one basket; it's about understanding the baskets you have and how you can use them to support your acquisition. It requires a thorough analysis of your financial situation, an understanding of the risks involved, and a clear-eyed view of the potential rewards.

It's about creativity. Perhaps you'll use a combination of these equity sources, crafting a funding mosaic that minimizes your risk while maximizing your potential for success. It's about looking at your assets not just as static figures on a balance sheet but as dynamic tools that can be wielded to shape your future.

As you contemplate the possibilities, remember that the use of personal equity is just one part of a broader financial strategy. It should be complemented with traditional funding sources like bank loans, seller financing, and perhaps even partnerships or private investors. This multi-faceted approach can not only distribute the risk but also open up opportunities that might otherwise remain out of reach

Chapter 7
IDENTIFYING DEAL PARTNERS

In this chapter, we will dig into the different types of professionals who can help you unearth the hidden gems in the complex and competitive world of business acquisitions. Whether you are looking to buy or sell a business, you will benefit from the expertise, guidance, and network of these deal partners, who can make the difference between striking gold and hitting a dead end. You will learn about the roles and responsibilities and how to pick the right ones for your situation. You will also discover how to work effectively with them, avoiding common pitfalls and maximizing your chances of closing a deal.

M&A Professionals

Let's take a moment to consider the scale of these professions. Compared to the approximately 4 million Realtors nationwide who facilitate residential and commercial real estate transactions, the number of Business Brokers or M&A Professionals stands at around 15,000. Despite this stark difference in numbers, this group shoulders the responsibility of an equally, if not more, complex transaction landscape.

M&A stewards are like miners in a gold rush. They sift through the dirt and rocks of a merger or acquisition, looking for the nuggets of value that others might miss. They must be proficient in financial analysis, comply with legal and regulatory standards, and have strong interpersonal skills to handle the needs and emotions of all parties involved. Their work starts with a careful evaluation of the business's worth, continues with the preparation of a detailed prospectus, and goes through the phases of deal screening, negotiation, and transaction closure.

The critical role of these stewards cannot be overstated. They are the bridge between buyers seeking to acquire a business that aligns with their strategic goals and sellers who wish to exit the market. Without their guidance, buyers could overpay, miss red flags in due diligence, or fail to acquire the necessary financing. Sellers, on the other hand, may undervalue their business, overlook key selling points, or fall into legal pitfalls.

The risks of the DIY method in buying a business are numerous. It's a path fraught with potential missteps. Buyers may inadvertently violate confidentiality agreements, misjudge the market, or fail to negotiate effectively. The absence of a skilled intermediary can lead to deals falling apart, sometimes after months of effort, or post-acquisition surprises that could cost both parties dearly.

These stewards bring to the table a wealth of industry-specific knowledge. They understand market trends, can accurately value a business, have a network of potential sellers, and can navigate complex negotiations. These professionals are adept at preparing a buyer for acquisition, which often includes making strategic adjustments to enhance their offer and attractiveness to sellers.

They provide an objective perspective that is invaluable in high-stakes situations. Emotions can run high when a buyer is acquiring a company that could transform their future. A broker serves as a buffer and can approach negotiations without the emotional investment that a buyer might have, leading to more rational decision-making.

Representing the buyer in a business acquisition is a complex and challenging task that requires a great steward to have a set of essential skills. These skills include:

- **Analytical Skills**: Can analyze vast amounts of data and information, such as financial statements, market reports, industry trends, and valuation models. They can interpret these data and draw meaningful insights that can guide the buyer's strategy and decision-making. Also assess the strengths and weaknesses of potential targets and identify opportunities and threats.

- **Communication Skills**: Can communicate effectively with various stakeholders, such as the buyer, the seller, other intermediaries, and professional advisors. They can convey complex information in a clear and concise manner, using appropriate language and tone. Also listen actively and attentively, understanding the needs, interests, and concerns of each party. Build rapport and trust with their clients and counterparts, as well as handle difficult or sensitive situations diplomatically.

- **Negotiation Skills**: Negotiate skillfully and confidently on behalf of the buyer. They can prepare a compelling offer, present it persuasively, and respond to counteroffers and objections. Balance the buyer's objectives and expectations with the seller's demands and constraints.

They can create value for both sides and achieve a mutually beneficial outcome. Also manage conflict and resolve impasses, as well as cope with pressure and uncertainty.

Legal Expertise

The importance of legal counsel is evident from the onset of a transaction. At the initial stage, lawyers conduct a thorough due diligence process, vetting every aspect of the target company. This scrutiny encompasses financial audits, compliance checks, and the assessment of contracts and liabilities. It is a meticulous process aimed at uncovering any potential legal pitfalls that could jeopardize the deal or haunt the acquirer post-merger.

Once due diligence is complete, the lawyer's function transitions into crafting the structure of the deal. This is where legal creativity comes into play. Attorneys must design agreements that not only reflect the commercial objectives of their clients but also anticipate and mitigate risks. They navigate through a labyrinth of regulations and laws to ensure that the transaction adheres to legal standards, thus safeguarding the parties involved against future disputes or regulatory backlash.

Negotiations are another critical phase where lawyers shine. They are the architects of the deal's terms and conditions, often finding innovative solutions to bridge gaps between the parties' expectations. Adept M&A lawyers use their expertise to negotiate warranties, indemnities, and other contractual protections that serve as armor against unforeseen liabilities.

Lawyers are pivotal in managing the transaction's risks. They assess and advise on the implications of market conditions, tax considerations, and potential antitrust issues. With their expertise, they can predict scenarios that could unravel the deal and take preemptive measures to avert such outcomes.

Protecting client interests is, perhaps, the most personal role lawyers play in takeovers. Whether it's ensuring that the seller receives fair compensation and is released from future obligations or that the buyer acquires a clean title to the assets, the lawyer is the steadfast champion of their client's rights. They pore over every clause, every representation, ensuring that their client's interests are paramount and shielded throughout the process.

Post-merger integration is a challenging phase, and lawyers play a vital role in it. They help merge different corporate cultures, unify legal entities, and facilitate the transfer of contracts and licenses. Their carefulness in this phase is essential for an easy transition and the achievement of the deal's expected benefits.

Accountants and Tax Consultants

Imagine two companies, each with their unique financial DNA, coming together. The complexities are immense. It's not merely about legal compliance or ticking off checklists. It's about peering into the fiscal heart of an enterprise and ensuring that what beats there is healthy, sustainable, and capable of thriving post-merger. Accountants and CPAs step in with their forensic tools to dissect financial statements, evaluate assets and liabilities, and sniff out any potential risks that might lurk in the shadows of balance sheets.

Tax planning, meanwhile, is the delicate operation that can unearth or bury valuable resources. Tax rules of merger transactions are complex and variable. The role of a tax consultant is like that of a skilled miner extracting precious metals from the ore. They must evaluate the tax impact of the deal, recommend the best way to structure the acquisition, and find opportunities for tax optimization. It's a challenge of complying with the regulations while ensuring the profitability of the entity.

Due diligence is another critical area where accountants shine. They dig deep into the financial workings of the target company, assessing everything from revenue and profit trends to the sustainability of cash flows and the robustness of internal financial controls. This financial detective work serves as the foundation upon which sound investment decisions are made. It's about verifying claims, challenging assumptions, and ensuring that the price paid for an acquisition is supported by the underlying economic realities.

Accountants and CPAs are the unsung heroes of deals. Their work is meticulous, often conducted away from the glamour of headline-grabbing announcements. Yet, the value they add is immeasurable.

In every acquisition transaction, there lies a story of transformation, and it is the accountant's hand that helps write this narrative. They not only crunch numbers but also craft strategies that drive businesses forward. They are not just keepers of financial records but also guardians of fiscal prudence.

Wealth Management

A wealth manager is not merely a financial advisor but a strategic ally in the safeguarding and growth of your post-acquisition wealth. Their expertise extends beyond investment advice into the realms of tax planning, estate management, and often, life coaching. They are the architects of your financial future, ensuring that the wealth you've accumulated works for you, aligning with your personal goals and values.

Their function is multifaceted; wealth managers have a keen eye for the financial ecosystem and understand how various elements interact. They consider the implications of the acquisition on your overall financial picture and strategize accordingly. It's their job to anticipate market shifts, identify potential risks, and advise on diversification strategies that will protect and grow your wealth in the long term.

Post-acquisition wealth management starts with understanding the liquidity event. This can be a complex and emotional time, as it often involves significant changes to your financial status and the need to make decisions that will impact your future. A wealth manager helps to navigate this landscape by assessing your new financial position and creating a structured plan to manage your capital effectively.

This includes devising strategies for reinvestment. With a large influx of funds, the temptation to immediately indulge in extravagant purchases can be strong. However, a seasoned wealth manager will provide guidance on how to invest wisely, ensuring that your wealth is not just preserved but also has the potential to grow. They will introduce investment opportunities that align with your risk tolerance and long-term objectives, whether that's funding startups, entering into real estate, or exploring other asset classes like art or philanthropic ventures.

Another critical element is tax planning. The consequences of a merger transaction on your tax situation can be profound.

A wealth manager works with tax professionals to help you understand the nuances of your new tax obligations and to develop strategies that minimize your tax liabilities. This might involve setting up trusts, charitable giving, or taking advantage of tax-efficient investment vehicles.

Estate planning also becomes an immediate priority. The newly acquired wealth must be protected and structured in a way that it can be passed on to future generations according to your wishes. This often involves complex legal and financial planning, but a good wealth manager will guide you through the process, ensuring that your legacy is secured.

Wealth managers can also offer counsel on life beyond the deal. Acquiring wealth is one thing, but finding fulfillment and purpose in life with that wealth is another challenge entirely. They may help you explore passions or ventures that provide meaning, ensuring that your financial success translates to a rich and satisfying life.

In essence, wealth managers are the unsung heroes of the M&A aftermath. They play a pivotal role in ensuring that the financial success of a deal translates into long-term prosperity and well-being for their clients. Their work often goes unnoticed in the public eye, but it is crucial for those who have undergone the transformative experience of a merger or acquisition.

Choosing:
Business Brokers vs. Investment Bankers

Business brokers are the navigators of the small to mid-sized business sales. They are akin to real estate agents for companies, connecting sellers with buyers and facilitating transactions that might otherwise fly under the radar. These brokers excel in handling Main Street deals, where the companies in question often have a valuation of under $5 million. They are the boots on the ground for the small business owner, providing a personalized touch, local market knowledge, and an understanding of the nuances specific to smaller scale operations.

They are typically involved in the end-to-end process, from valuing the business to marketing it, negotiating terms, and steering the deal to a close. Their fees are often structured as a commission on the sale price, making them highly motivated to secure the best possible deal for their clients.

In contrast, investment bankers play in the big leagues. They operate on a larger scale, handling complex transactions for companies with values often exceeding $50 million. Investment bankers bring a wealth of knowledge in financial modeling, structuring deals, and leveraging their extensive networks to find suitable merger or acquisition targets. They are masters of capital markets, equipped to advise on and facilitate not only M&A but also initial public offerings, raising capital, and other significant financial maneuvers.

A key differentiator is their approach to fees; investment bankers typically charge both a deposit and a royalty, aligning their interests with their clients but also ensuring they are rewarded for their time and expertise regardless of the outcome. They are the mine managers, ensuring each section of the excavation process is efficient and delivering a profitable yield.

When deciding between a business broker and an investment banker, consider the size and complexity of your deal. For a local business owner looking to retire and pass on the reins to a new owner, a business broker's local insights and hands-on approach can be invaluable. However, for a rapidly scaling tech startup seeking to merge with a multinational corporation, the strategic advisory and broad reach of an investment banker are indispensable.

It's not just about the size of the company but also about the complexity of the transaction. If your business has intricate financial structures, diverse product lines across various markets, or you're looking for a cross-border deal, the sophisticated services of an investment banker are often required to navigate these complexities.

Understanding the strengths of each advisor is crucial. Business brokers are often adept at understanding the personal side of business – the legacy of a family-owned company, the impact of the sales on employees, and the continuity of the business post-sale. Investment bankers, with their analytical prowess, excel in maximizing shareholder value, identifying synergies between merging entities, and crafting deals that enhance financial and strategic positioning.

The suitability of the advisor also extends to their network and reach. Business brokers may have a vast network within a particular region or industry, making them ideal for deals that require a deep understanding of local market dynamics. Investment bankers, with their global contacts, can tap into international markets, find buyers or sellers who are out of reach for business brokers, and create bidding wars that drive up the sale price.

Chapter 8
DIGGING FOR GOLD

In the ever-evolving business landscape, a handful of Texas-born companies have emerged as trailblazers, forging their paths through strategic acquisitions and unwavering determination. From humble beginnings as small enterprises, these giants have defied the odds, expanded their reach and solidified their positions as industry leaders.

Imagine a small business owner in Texas, eager to expand but unsure of the best path forward. Through the lens of several successful companies—7-Eleven, Inc., Fluor Corporation, Whole Foods Market, Dell Technologies, Brinker International, Inc., Cinemark Holdings, Inc., and GameStop Corp.—we explore how strategic acquisitions can transform a modest enterprise into an industry leader.

Acquisition Trailblazers - Texas Titans

7-Eleven, Inc.: The Convenience Giant
- Founder: Joe C. Thompson Sr.
- Where Founded: Dallas, Texas
- Industry: Convenience Stores and Retail

- History: Founded in 1927 as Tote'm Stores, 7-Eleven revolutionized the retail industry by operating longer hours and offering a wide range of products. The name was changed in 1946 to reflect its new hours of 7 a.m. to 11 p.m.
- Growth Through Acquisition: Over the decades, 7-Eleven grew by acquiring smaller convenience stores and franchises. Key acquisitions included White Hen Pantry and TETCO in the 2010s, which significantly expanded its market presence.
- Current Status: Private
- Founder's Involvement: Joe C. Thompson Sr. passed away, but his legacy continues through the brand. The company is currently owned by Seven & I Holdings Co., a Japanese retail group.

Lessons for Small Business Owners: Strategic acquisitions can rapidly scale operations, diversify offerings, and enter new markets. For 7-Eleven, acquiring established local stores allowed for quick market penetration and brand recognition.

Fluor Corporation: Engineering Excellence

- Founder: John Simon Fluor
- Where Founded: Dallas, Texas
- Industry: Engineering and Construction
- History: Founded in 1912, Fluor Corporation began as a small construction firm and evolved into a global engineering and construction leader.
- Growth Through Acquisition: Fluor expanded its capabilities and global reach by acquiring companies like Stork (2015), which provided industrial services, and Goar, Allison & Associates (2003), which enhanced its engineering solutions.

- Current Status: Publicly traded (NYSE: FLR)
- Founder's Involvement: John Simon Fluor is no longer involved as he passed away, but the company continues to thrive, building on his legacy.

Lessons for Small Business Owners: By acquiring companies with complementary strengths, businesses can enhance their service offerings and enter new sectors. For Fluor, this strategy facilitated its growth into a global engineering leader.

Whole Foods Market: Revolutionizing Grocery Retail

- Founders: John Mackey, Renee Lawson Hardy, Craig Weller, and Mark Skiles
- Where Founded: Austin, Texas
- Industry: Grocery and Organic Food Retail
- History: Founded in 1980, Whole Foods Market focused on providing organic and natural foods, pioneering the natural food industry.
- Growth Through Acquisition: Whole Foods expanded by acquiring other natural food stores, including Wellspring Grocery (1991) and Wild Oats Markets (2007). These acquisitions allowed Whole Foods to dominate the organic food market.
- Current Status: Acquired by Amazon in 2017, now operates as a subsidiary.
- Founder's Involvement: John Mackey remained with the company until his retirement in 2022.

Lessons for Small Business Owners: Acquiring businesses with similar values and customer bases can streamline growth and strengthen market position. Whole Foods used this approach to become a leading name in organic retail.

Dell Technologies: From Dorm Room to Global Tech Leader

- Founder: Michael Dell
- Where Founded: Austin, Texas
- Industry: Technology, Computer Hardware, and Services
- History: Founded in 1984 in Michael Dell's dorm room at the University of Texas, Austin, Dell Technologies began by selling PCs directly to consumers, which was revolutionary at the time.
- Growth Through Acquisition: Dell's strategic acquisitions included Perot Systems (2009) to enhance IT services and EMC Corporation (2016) to enter the data storage market. These moves diversified Dell's portfolio and expanded its technological capabilities.
- Current Status: Publicly traded (NYSE: DELL)
- Founder's Involvement: Michael Dell is still actively involved, serving as Chairman and CEO.

Lessons for Small Business Owners: Diversifying through acquisitions can protect against market volatility and foster innovation. Dell's strategy demonstrates the power of evolving from a single product line to a comprehensive tech powerhouse.

Brinker International, Inc.: A Culinary Empire

- Founder: Norman Brinker
- Where Founded: Dallas, Texas
- Industry: Restaurant and Hospitality
- History: Brinker International started with one Chili's Grill & Bar location in 1975, focusing on casual dining.
- Growth Through Acquisition: Brinker expanded by acquiring restaurant brands like Romano's Macaroni

Grill (1989) and Maggiano's Little Italy (1995). These acquisitions helped Brinker offer a variety of dining experiences.
- Current Status: Publicly traded (NYSE: EAT)
- Founder's Involvement: Norman Brinker passed away in 2009, but his impact on the company and the industry remains significant.

Lessons for Small Business Owners: Expanding through acquiring complementary brands can attract diverse customer segments and create multiple revenue streams. Brinker's strategy shows how a small restaurant can grow into a multi-brand dining empire.

Cinemark Holdings, Inc.: Dominating the Cinema Industry

- Founder: Lee Roy Mitchell
- Where Founded: Plano, Texas
- Industry: Movie Theaters and Entertainment
- History: Founded in 1984, Cinemark aimed to offer a superior movie-going experience.
- Growth Through Acquisition: Cinemark grew by acquiring smaller theater chains, including Century Theatres (2006) and Rave Cinemas (2013). These acquisitions expanded its geographic reach and market share.
- Current Status: Publicly traded (NYSE: CNK)
- Founder's Involvement: Lee Roy Mitchell continues to be involved as Chairman Emeritus.

Lessons for Small Business Owners: Acquiring competitors can eliminate market fragmentation and increase customer base. Cinemark's growth illustrates the importance of consolidation in achieving market dominance.

GameStop Corp.: From Small Retailer to Gaming Giant

- Founders: James McCurry and Gary M. Kusin
- Where Founded: Dallas, Texas
- Industry: Video Game and Electronics Retail
- History: Founded in 1984 as Babbage's, GameStop began as a small software retailer before expanding into video games.
- Growth Through Acquisition: GameStop expanded by acquiring game retailers like Electronics Boutique (2005) and Micromania (2008). These acquisitions allowed it to dominate the gaming retail market.
- Current Status: Publicly traded (NYSE: GME)
- Founder's Involvement: Founders are no longer involved, and the company has undergone significant changes, particularly with the rise of digital gaming.

Lessons for Small Business Owners: Strategic acquisitions can help a business adapt to industry changes and maintain market relevance. GameStop's expansion through acquiring gaming-focused stores solidified its position as a leading retailer.

These stories highlight the transformative power of strategic acquisitions. By learning from these industry leaders, small business owners can understand the potential of acquisitions to drive growth, diversify offerings, and achieve market dominance. Whether it's through consolidating local competitors or expanding into new sectors, the path to significant growth often involves bold acquisition strategies.

These companies, once small businesses with humble beginnings, have defied the odds and transformed into industry giants through a strategic combination of organic growth and well-executed acquisitions. Their stories serve as inspiration for entrepreneurs and business leaders alike, showcasing the power of vision, perseverance, and the willingness to seize opportunities for growth through acquisitions.

Chapter 9
ACQUISITION ADVANTAGE

The term "Mergers & Acquisition" may conjure up images of corporate titans joining forces or swallowing up their rivals in a bid to dominate the market. But this is only one aspect of M&A, and not necessarily the most common or profitable one. In fact, many experts prefer to call it the small "m" and big "A" in M&A, because the real advantage lies in acquisition, especially in the small business sector.

Acquisition is the act of buying an existing business that has a proven track record of success, cash flow, and profitability. It's not about gambling on an uncertain future; it's about investing in a solid present. It's not about starting from scratch; it's about building on what's already there. It's not about searching for a needle in a haystack; it's about mining for gold in a rich vein.

In this book, we will show you why to use acquisition as a powerful tool to transform your financial future and create lasting value for yourself and your stakeholders. Whether you're an existing business owner looking to scale up, a first-time buyer looking to start your entrepreneurial journey, or an investor looking for new opportunities, we will guide you through the process.

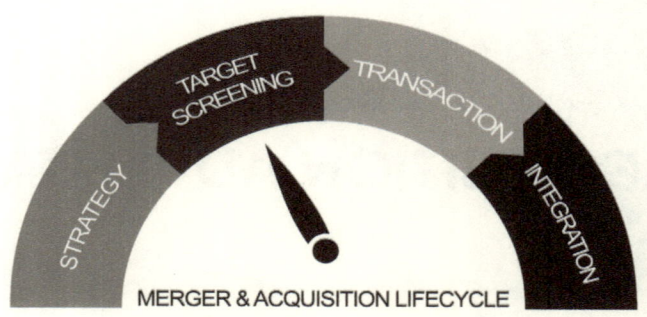

We will also share with you the stories of real-life acquirers who have used this strategy to achieve their goals and overcome their challenges. You will learn from their successes and mistakes, and discover how they have leveraged acquisition to create synergies, growth, and wealth.

It's time to take the plunge and explore the hidden treasures of the small business sector. It's time to reap the benefits of acquisition.

Journey to Financial Transformation

Small businesses are more than the quaint shops and family-owned restaurants lining Main Street; they are the backbone of the economy. They generate nearly half of U.S. economic activity and create a significant share of new jobs. This figure reflects their importance and influence. They stimulate growth, drive competition, and foster innovation.

But there's more to small businesses than just their economic contributions. Over 65% of these enterprises are profitable, revealing a landscape ripe for investment and growth. It's here, in the fertile ground of business profitability, that acquisition emerges as a powerful tool for financial transformation.

The concept of buying cash flow might sound simple, yet it's a profound strategy that underpins small business takeovers. It's the act of acquiring a business whose revenue streams are established and consistent, offering immediate financial benefits to the buyer. This approach is less about speculation and more about securing a foothold in a market with a business model that's already proven successful.

When you consider acquisition in the small business context, it's not just a means of expansion but a strategic maneuver that can redefine a business's trajectory. It can offer an existing small business the chance to scale operations, access new markets, or acquire competencies and technologies that would take years to develop organically.

The beauty of mergers and acquisition lies in its accessibility. It's not reserved for the elite with vast reserves of capital; it's a viable option for the many, not just the few. With the right strategy, a transaction can be financed through a combination of cash, loans, and seller financing, making it a reality for those who are ready to take the leap.

Acquisition is also a way to tap into the hidden goldmines of the small business sector. For an owner, acquiring another company can uncover new sources of revenue and profit in different markets and products. But more than that, it can create value by combining the strengths and resources of both businesses, resulting in synergies that can boost efficiency, reduce costs, and expand market share. It's an opportunity to transform both the acquired and the acquiring business, creating benefits for employees, customers, and communities alike.

However, digging for treasure in the small business sector is not a simple task. It demands careful research, a keen eye for the market, and the skill to merge different business cultures and systems. But for those who have the courage and the tools to explore this terrain, the rewards can be substantial.

The narrative of small business acquisition is one of opportunity and transformation. It's a story about leveraging what's already working and building on it to create something even more successful. It's about recognizing the potential in the small business sector and using acquisition as a catalyst to unlock that potential.

Benefits of Acquisition

But it's not just about size and reach; it's about synergy. The combined efforts and resources of two companies can lead to greater efficiency, innovation, and productivity. Through acquisition, a company can access new technologies and expertise that may have been out of reach or would have taken years to develop internally. These synergies can lead to cost savings and enhanced profitability, ultimately benefiting shareholders and stakeholders alike.

"Companies are not set in stone. It's not all-or-nothing. It's possible to make things better incrementally, and acquisitions can be a big part of that process." Elon Musk, CEO of SpaceX and Tesla. Acquisition can be a strategic move to neutralize competition. By acquiring a rival, a company can eliminate a competitive threat and consolidate its position in the industry. This doesn't just mean less competition; it often translates into stronger bargaining power with suppliers, better terms with distributors, and greater influence in the industry.

Risk management is another compelling benefit of acquisition. Diversification through acquisition can help a company spread its risks across different markets, products, or services. If one part of the business faces challenges, the others can potentially offset the impact, providing a cushion that can be crucial in volatile times.

Now, aligning acquisition strategy with investor objectives is paramount. Investors seek growth, stability, returns, and acquisitions when executed well can deliver on these fronts. A well-chosen acquisition can provide the acceleration needed to meet aggressive growth targets, while also offering the stability that comes from a larger, more diverse operation.

Appeal of Cash-Flow

Think about this remarkable fact: an astonishing 72% of business owners, whose revenues range from $250,000 to $20 million, run their businesses without an exit strategy. They're deeply involved in the daily operations, leaving them unaware of the future of their business journey. This oversight creates a fertile ground for the savvy buyer. It's a situation where opportunity and readiness meet, offering a rare opportunity to take over a business ready for transition, where cash flow is already a friend, not a foe you're trying to win over.

Starting a business from scratch is akin to digging for gold in a barren land. It's a risky and exhausting endeavor, with unknown obstacles and rewards shrouded in doubt. You're exploring new territory, convincing every prospect, one by one, of your value. As any startup founder knows, starting a new business takes more than money, but also grit. The odds of success are low and often quoted, with many new businesses collapsing soon after they launch. On the flip side, acquiring an established business is like entering a forest of towering trees. The ground is fertile; the ecosystem is thriving, and your role shifts from sowing to nurturing and expanding. The customer base is established, the brand is recognized, and perhaps most importantly, the cash flow is consistent. The initial investment may be higher, but so is the predictability of return on investment.

On the other hand, buying an established business is like mining a rich vein of ore. The land is already proven; the mine is operational, and your role changes from prospecting to extracting and refining. The customer base is loyal, the brand is trusted, and perhaps most importantly, the cash flow is steady. The initial investment may be higher, but so is the certainty of return on investment.

The secret that underpins this strategy is not just in the acquisition but in the meticulous selection and integration process. It's about recognizing that not all businesses are equal and that due diligence is your unwavering ally. It's about understanding the market, the business's position within it, and the potential for growth. It's about evaluating systems, processes, and teams — ensuring that what you're stepping into can be sustained and scaled.

Yet, the acquisition is not merely a financial transaction; it's a human one. It means stepping into a narrative already in motion, one that involves employees, customers, and the legacy of the previous owner. The successful acquirer navigates this transition with grace, respecting what has been built while steering the business towards new horizons.

The benefits of buying into an existing cash flow are manifold. You leapfrog the perilous startup phase, bypass the need for immediate market validation, and perhaps most enticingly, you may reap the rewards of cash flow from day one. The lessons learned from the past owner can become your steppingstones to further success, and the established relationships with suppliers and clients can prove invaluable.

Yet, with these benefits come responsibilities. You must be adept at identifying the right business to buy, understanding its true worth, and negotiating a fair purchase price. Post-acquisition, the challenge shifts to maintaining the business's successful trajectory while implementing improvements and innovations to foster growth.

The path of acquiring a cash-flowing business is not without its hurdles, but for those equipped with strategic acumen, it's a path that can lead to accelerated success. It's about recognizing that while the entrepreneurial spirit is often associated with exploring new frontiers, there's profound wisdom in building upon the rich deposits left by others.

The Power of Stability

Consider the timeline to profitability—a critical measure of a business's success. Startups, fueled by optimism and venture capital, may take anywhere from three to five years to reach profitability if they survive that long. Throughout this period, they burn through cash, pivot, and iterate, all while trying to carve out a niche in the market.

On the other hand, an acquired business can often achieve profitability within the first one to two years under new ownership. This isn't magic; it's the result of leveraging an existing business model that already generates revenue. By streamlining operations, expanding market reach, or introducing incremental innovations, new owners can accelerate growth and profitability without reinventing the wheel.

Acquiring a business also means that you inherit a team—a group of individuals who are already familiar with the business operations, the market, and the customers. The value of an experienced team cannot be overstressed. They are the tools that keep the mine running smoothly and can provide invaluable insights into business dynamics that are not easily replicable.

Furthermore, established businesses come with established relationships. Suppliers, distributors, and even competitors know the business, making it easier to negotiate terms and understand the market landscape. These relationships can take years to build from scratch. They are not just conduits for transactions; they are strategic assets that can open doors to new opportunities and partnerships.

Financial institutions and investors also look favorably upon established businesses with a solid track record. Obtaining financing becomes less of an uphill battle as the business's financials speak for themselves. This access to capital is critical for growth and expansion and can be a bottleneck for startups that lack collateral or a proven revenue model.

However, it's not just about the numbers. Acquiring an established business can also be a more palatable journey for the entrepreneur. The trials and tribulations of startup life are well-documented—the long hours, the uncertainty, and the constant need for innovation and adaptation. While these are also aspects of running an acquired business, there is generally a clearer path to follow, one with fewer existential threats and more predictable outcomes.

In the end, it's about leveraging what already works and making it better. It's about recognizing the value in the tried and true and using it as a springboard for further success. This approach might not have the romantic appeal of the startup narrative, but it has a pragmatic appeal that is hard to ignore.

Faster Route to Profits

The immediate financial benefits of acquiring a cash-flowing business are numerous and noteworthy. Unlike a startup, where the climb to profitability can be rocky with uncertainty, an existing business offers a mine that's already been discovered. It's a scenario where the previous owner has done the hard work of digging the ore, and you, as the new miner, simply step into the site and extract the gold.

"We are unashamedly aggressive in our pursuit of doing business and, to that end, mergers and acquisitions are a key part of our strategy." Larry Page, Co-founder of Google.

One of the most significant advantages is the existing customer base. It's no secret that startups can take years to build a solid customer foundation. Those initial one to two years are a critical period during which many businesses falter, primarily due to the lack of a loyal customer base. When you acquire a business that's already in motion, you're not just buying assets or inventory; you're inheriting a customer base that has already been mined.

These customers are the essence of the business, providing immediate revenue streams. The relationships established with them can often extend beyond the transactional, with loyalty and trust built over time. This existing customer loyalty can be a goldmine. Rather than spending countless hours and significant financial resources on marketing to attract a new audience, you can focus on expanding and enhancing the relationships with your current customers.

Moreover, a cash-flowing business provides instant insights into the market. Sales data, customer feedback, and performance metrics are at your fingertips from day one, allowing for strategic decisions to be made with a level of confidence that a new entrepreneur can only dream of. This data isn't just historical; it's a real-time snapshot of what's working and what's not, enabling you to pivot and adapt swiftly to maintain and grow your profitability.

The operational infrastructure of an existing business is another valuable ore in this quest for immediate returns. The systems for delivering products or services, from extraction to refinement, have been proven in the field. You inherit a blueprint of sorts, one that's been polished through experimentation. This means you can spend less time drilling for solutions and more time expanding and enhancing.

Now, let's talk about the financial aspect. Acquiring a business usually comes with established revenue streams. This means that from the moment you sign on the dotted line, the business is generating cash flow. There's no waiting period to break even or turn a profit; it's happening as you take the reins. This immediate cash flow can then be reinvested back into the business to fuel growth or used to service the debt incurred in the purchase, thereby reducing financial risk.

In addition to revenue, there's also the matter of cost savings. An existing business may have long-standing relationships with suppliers and vendors, which can translate into lower costs for goods and services due to bulk purchasing or loyalty discounts. These savings can bolster profit margins and give you a competitive edge in pricing your offerings to the market.

The Key to Success

The business landscape is riddled with tales of mergers and acquisitions that either propelled companies to new heights or led them into a quagmire of financial loss. What distinguishes the former from the latter is often the presence of a meticulously crafted strategic plan. Strategic planning in a deal involves analyzing potential synergies, understanding market dynamics, evaluating strategic fit, and much more.

Now, to truly grasp the importance of strategic planning, we must appreciate the core equation of value creation. In its simplest form, the value of a business can be broken down into three components: Profit, Seller Discretionary Earnings (SDE)/Owner Benefits, and Assets. Each element plays a critical role in painting the full picture of a business's worth.

Profit, the most basic of the three, is the financial gain realized when revenue exceeds expenses. It is the heartbeat of any business, reflecting its ability to generate cash and sustain operations. However, profit alone doesn't capture the full value of a business. This is where Seller Discretionary Earnings come into play. SDE represents the economic benefit to the owner, which includes the profit plus any perks or additional income that the owner might receive. It's a more personalized view of a business's financial health, one that considers the owner's unique influence on the company's earnings.

Lastly, we must consider Assets. Assets are the tangible and intangible items that a business owns, which can range from physical machinery and inventory to patents and brand recognition. They form the foundation of the company, undergirding its operations and providing value in their own right.

Strategic planning in the context of a merger requires an intricate dance between these three elements. It's about enhancing profit through operational efficiencies, maximizing SDE by identifying and leveraging the unique strengths of the business, and optimizing the value of assets by ensuring they are effectively utilized or strategically divested.

But strategic planning is more than just numbers. It's about envisioning a future where two entities come together to create something greater than the sum of their parts. It's about understanding that the success of an acquisition deal hinges on the seamless integration of cultures, systems, and visions. It requires a leader to look beyond the spreadsheets and see the human element, recognizing that people are the driving force behind any successful deal.

"You have to be willing to have the hard conversations and make the tough calls. Sometimes, that means pursuing mergers and acquisitions to drive growth." Indra Nooyi, Former CEO of PepsiCo.

Consider a technology firm acquiring a smaller startup. The strategic plan might highlight the startup's innovative products as key assets, the potential for profit through expanded market reach, and the SDE through the startup founder's expertise. But the plan should also address how to integrate the startup's agile culture with the larger firm's established processes. This is the kind of comprehensive thinking that fuels value creation in takeover.

In crafting a strategic plan for takeover, leaders must be vigilant, adaptive, and constantly in tune with the evolving business environment. They should engage in thorough due diligence, not just to uncover potential risks but also to identify hidden opportunities. They should establish clear goals, set realistic timelines, and foster strong communication across all levels of both organizations.

Let's not underestimate the power of strategic planning. It's the compass that guides companies through the complexities of deals, ensuring that they don't lose sight of their destination amidst the tumult of negotiations. It's the blueprint for value creation, the roadmap that charts the course from where a company is to where it aspires to be.

Scope and Location Flexibility

Let's begin by dissecting the deal scope. It's a balancing act: on one side, the allure of multiple deals promises diversified risks and greater reach; on the other, each deal requires resources, time, and attention. Your funding capacity is the cornerstone here. It's not merely about the capital you have on hand but understanding the flow of cash and the ability to sustain operations post-acquisition. You must assess your financial reservoirs and have a clear strategy for maintaining liquidity.

It's tempting to pursue every opportunity that comes knocking, yet the savvy investor knows that restraint often pays off. One must consider not only the initial investment but also the hidden costs—integration challenges, cultural alignments, and potential value creation. Each deal must be scrutinized for its ability to align with the long-term strategy, and sometimes saying no is the most profitable move.

Now, let's pivot to location considerations. The digital age has blurred the lines of physical boundaries, making it possible for businesses to operate virtually anywhere. However, location still matters. It can influence everything from customer access and talent acquisition to regulatory landscapes and tax implications.

When evaluating potential acquisitions, consider whether you're looking for a stronghold in a familiar market or expansion into uncharted territories. Each route has its merits. A local focus might provide a deeper understanding of the consumer base and established networks, while casting a wider geographical net could tap into new demographics and diversify market risks.

However, don't be swayed by the glamor of an international presence without considering the practicalities. Language barriers, cultural differences, and time zones can complicate operations. Moreover, local laws and regulations can present hurdles that are not only difficult to navigate but can also impact profitability.

The key is to establish a clear understanding of what you can handle and where you can thrive. It might mean starting with a series of small, local deals to build a solid foundation before taking the leap into a larger, more complex, international acquisition. Or, if your infrastructure supports it, you might leapfrog to a strategic position in a foreign market that aligns with your growth ambitions.

In every decision, remember that the ultimate goal is not just to acquire but to enhance, grow, and create a sustainable and profitable business model. Each deal should be a building block towards that end, not a stray piece that doesn't fit the puzzle.

Consider the case of a mid-sized company that leveraged its strong regional presence to acquire a competitor. The acquisition not only eliminated a market rival but also provided economies of scale, allowing the company to negotiate better prices from suppliers and streamline operations. This move was strategic, well within the company's financial capabilities, and focused on its established market, ensuring integration was smooth and value was quickly realized.

Example of Value

In the dynamic landscape of modern business, the strategy of mergers and acquisitions (M&A) stands out as a beacon of opportunity for the savvy investor or entrepreneur. When we talk about practical examples of business valuation and investment requirements, what we're really examining is the process of understanding the worth of a business and the necessary financial steps to take it under one's wing.

Let's delve into this through tangible examples, analyzing two hypothetical businesses priced at $500,000 and $1,000,000, respectively. We'll dissect the components of down payment, seller discretionary earnings (SDE), and cash flow (C/F) to demystify the calculations and strategies behind successful business acquisitions.

Firstly, let's consider a business valued at half a million dollars. In the merger world, this could very well be a solid, small-to-medium-sized business with a stable customer base and a robust SDE. Seller Discretionary Earnings are the profits left after the cost of goods sold and critical operating expenses are subtracted. These earnings are pivotal in determining the business's health and potential for growth. For a $500,000 business, an SDE might range anywhere from $100,000 to $200,000 annually, depending on the industry and the efficiency of operations. This figure is crucial for understanding what kind of cash flow the business can generate for a potential buyer.

For most small business acquisitions, buyers can anticipate a down payment requirement of 10-20%. So, for our $500,000 business, you'd be looking at a down payment between $50,000 and $100,000. The cash flow, or the net amount of cash being transferred into and out of the business, should comfortably cover the loan payments for the remaining purchase price, while still providing a reasonable return on investment (ROI) for the buyer.

As we escalate to a business with a $1,000,000 price tag, the financial dynamics shift, but the fundamental principles remain the same. With a business of this caliber, you might expect a higher SDE, possibly in the ballpark of $300,000 to $500,000. The down payment, following the same percentage range, could be $100,000 to $200,000. Again, the cash flow must be enough to service the debt incurred from the purchase and to ensure that the investor sees a profitable return.

The beauty of these figures lies not in their complexity but in their simplicity. They provide a clear road map for investors to assess the feasibility of an acquisition. By analyzing the SDE, you can gauge the business's profitability; by considering the down payment, you can determine the upfront investment required; and by understanding the cash flow, you can project the ongoing financial health of the business post-acquisition.

In the quest to acquire a business, it's essential to recognize that these numbers are not just arbitrary figures but the core of the investment decision. They reveal a vein of potential, risk, and reward. A business with an attractive SDE and healthy cash flow is like a rich ore ready for the extraction. It promises the investor a stream of income that can pay off the initial investment and continue to provide financial benefits for years to come.

M&A strategies are not just about numbers, though. They're about vision and execution. It's about seeing the latent potential in a business, understanding its true value, and having the acumen to increase that value post-acquisition. When you approach a business with the intent to merge or acquire, you're not just buying its current state; you're investing in its future – and, by extension, your own.

Chapter 10
MAIN STREET CASE STUDIES

Just as miners dig for precious metals and gems, entrepreneurs can mine for valuable opportunities in the form of acquisitions. Acquiring a business can be a rewarding way to grow your existing company, enter a new market, or diversify your portfolio. In this chapter, we will share some real-life examples of how entrepreneurs have struck gold by acquiring businesses and how they have leveraged their acquisitions to create lasting value.

1. Strategic Acquisition Path
From Sales Executive to Entrepreneur

Buyer Background

Meet John Reynolds, a seasoned sales professional with over 15 years of experience at a company specializing in copy machines. With a knack for sales, John once managed a team but found his true passion in direct sales, a role that afforded him a considerable income of over $250K annually, a flexible schedule, and ample family time. Married with two teenage kids,

John is also a dedicated churchgoer and enjoys woodworking in his spare time, a hobby that has seen him craft pieces for his home, church, and friends.

Despite a brush with the law in his younger years, John has turned his life around, establishing himself as a respected figure in his community and profession. Now, at the age of 45, he feels the itch to be his own boss and set his own path. He decided to channel his years of experience and substantial savings into acquiring a business.

Seller Background

The cabinet shop, located in the heart of DFW, Texas, had been owned by Mark for 17 years. Mark had started the business in his father's garage with just one piece of equipment, driven by his passion for woodworking and his desire to avoid working on Sundays, which would have been required had he pursued his initial plan to become a police officer. Over the years, Mark had grown the business to just under $3M in revenue, with a team of 16 employees, including his wife. They owned the property housing the business, and the company had a well-structured team consisting of a GM, foreman, builders, and installers, with Mark and his wife handling sales and back-office activities.

The Acquisition Journey

John's acquisition journey began with a clear vision: to leverage his sales acumen, managerial experience, and love for creating value into owning and running a business. Here's a step-by-step look at how John navigated this transition.

Step 1: Identifying the Right Business

Given his background, John knew that his strengths lay in sales, customer relationships, and team management.

He wanted a business where these skills would be pivotal to success. After some contemplation and research, he zeroed in on a small but profitable woodworking shop—a custom cabinet shop in Dallas-Fort Worth, Texas. This business was owned by the same individual for 17 years and had grown from humble beginnings in a garage to a company just shy of $3M in annual revenue, employing 16 people, including the owner's wife.

Step 2: Evaluating the Business

John conducted thorough due diligence, which included:

- **Financial Analysis**: Reviewing the shop's financial statements for the past five years to understand its profitability, cash flow, and any outstanding debts.

- **Market Position**: Assessing the shop's market position, customer base, and reputation.

- **Operational Efficiency**: Analyzing the shop's operations, including supplier relationships, inventory management, and production processes.

- **Growth Potential**: Identifying areas for growth, such as expanding the product line, increasing online presence, and enhancing marketing strategies.

Step 3: Understanding the Business Structure

The custom cabinet shop had a well-defined structure with a General Manager (GM), Foreman, Builders, and Installers. The owner and his wife handled the sales and back-office activities. The business primarily served commercial clients and had minimal residential work. Customers did not operate under recurring contracts but engaged the shop for individual jobs due to its excellent service.

Step 4: Securing Financing

John recognized that he needed additional financing to maintain sufficient working capital after the acquisition. He explored various financing options and ultimately secured an SBA loan. He structured the deal with a 10% down payment, a 5% seller financing note, and an SBA line of credit for working capital.

The seller financing note was a factor in obtaining the SBA loan, as it demonstrated the seller's confidence in the business and commitment to its success. It also provided John with more assurance that he would have the seller's support during the transition period. Also, reduced the risk of defaulting on the loan, as the seller would share the burden of any potential losses. The seller financing note also gave John some flexibility in terms of repayment, as he could negotiate the interest rate, term, and frequency of payments with the seller.

Step 5: Negotiating the Deal

John negotiated a fair purchase price based on the shop's current earnings, assets, and growth potential. The seller, an older gentleman ready to move on from the business he started after deciding not to pursue a career as a police officer due to religious commitments, was open to negotiation. They agreed on a combination of an upfront payment, a seller-financed portion, and the acquisition of the business's real estate.

Step 6: Transitioning into Ownership

To ensure a smooth transition, John spent the first few weeks shadowing the outgoing owner, learning the intricacies of the business, and meeting key customers and suppliers. The seller provided additional training and agreed to be available for consultation in the future.

Looking around the shop floor, John smiled as he watched the builders and installers working on various projects. He could already envision the improvements he wanted to make, the new markets he wanted to explore, and the legacy he hoped to build. With a deep breath and a sense of determination, John rolled up his sleeves and got to work, ready to unlock the full potential of his newly acquired business.

Step 7: Implementing Growth Strategies

Once fully in control, John implemented several growth strategies:

- **Expanding the Product Line**: Introduced new product offerings based on market trends and customer feedback.

- **Enhancing Online Presence**: Developed a comprehensive digital marketing strategy, including a new website, social media campaigns, and online sales channels.

- **Optimizing Operations**: Streamlined production processes and renegotiated supplier contracts to reduce costs and improve efficiency.

Outcome

Within two years, John transformed the small woodworking shop into a thriving business. His sales expertise and passion for woodworking helped him connect with customers on a personal level, driving repeat business and referrals. The shop's revenue doubled, and its online sales component grew significantly, establishing a robust new revenue stream.

John's journey from a high-earning sales executive to a successful business owner exemplifies the potential of strategic acquisition. By leveraging his skills, passion, and a well-thought-out plan, he was able to turn a new chapter in his professional life, achieving his dream of being his own boss while continuing to spend quality time with his family and contributing to his community.

2. Marketing Expert to Marketing Business Owner A Family's Path to Balance and Business Ownership

Buyer Background

Meet Laura Thompson, a seasoned marketing executive with a passion for community involvement and a growing family. As her two children became more active and required more of her time, Laura and her husband, Tom—an executive in the corporate finance arena—began to reassess their work-life balance. They wanted to provide a nurturing environment for their children, possibly even homeschooling them, while still fulfilling their professional aspirations.

Tom, who could work remotely, recognized the need for Laura to find a more flexible and fulfilling work arrangement. He wanted to empower her to live the life she desired, blending her professional expertise with her family commitments. The couple decided that acquiring a local business could offer the stability, flexibility, and proximity to home they sought.

Seller Background

In their search, Laura and Tom found a marketing company in a suburban area that serviced B2B clientele. The business was owned and operated by a husband and wife team, Mark and Sarah Williams. Mark, an ex-technology executive, provided technical support while Sarah, the marketing and people person, ran the company.

Their marketing company offered end-to-end services, including printing and mailing solutions for realtors and other commercial clients. The business had a steady stream of clients with no significant competition in the area. With in-house printing machines programmed by Mark and graphic design handled by Sarah, the company maintained a robust and reliable operation.

Mark and Sarah decided to sell the business as they wanted to move to Ohio to care for Mark's aging mother. They planned to use their savings to buy land and build a new home near her. The sale of the business would facilitate their move and allow them to focus on family.

The Acquisition Journey

Laura and Tom's acquisition journey began with a clear vision: to leverage Laura's marketing expertise and Tom's financial acumen into owning a business that would provide both professional fulfillment and personal flexibility. Here's a step-by-step look at how they navigated this transition.

Step 1: Identifying the Right Business

Laura and Tom wanted a business that matched Laura's skills in marketing and allowed for flexible hours. They discovered the marketing company owned by Mark and Sarah, which offered a perfect blend of established operations, local presence, and growth potential. The business's strong B2B clientele and comprehensive service offerings made it an attractive opportunity.

Interestingly, the business was in the same community where Laura and Tom lived. They had passed by the company's storefront numerous times and never knew that it could be the future for them. They were thrilled to find a local business that aligned with their vision and values.

Step 2: Evaluating the Business

Laura and Tom conducted thorough due diligence, which included:

- **Financial Analysis:** Reviewing the financial statements for the past five years to understand profitability, cash flow, and any outstanding debts.

- **Market Position:** Assessing the business's market position, customer base, and reputation.

- **Operational Efficiency:** Analyzing the business's operations, including equipment, maintenance schedules, and workflow processes.

- **Growth Potential:** Identifying areas for growth, such as expanding service offerings, enhancing online presence, and improving marketing strategies.

Step 3: Understanding the Business Structure

The marketing company had a simple yet efficient structure. Mark handled the technical aspects, such as programming the printing machines, while Sarah managed client relationships, graphic design, and overall business operations. This setup ensured high-quality service and customer satisfaction, with no significant competition in the area.

The seller's main advantage of not having any additional employees is the potential for greater profits. Without the added expenses of hiring and maintaining a team, the seller can keep more of the profits from each sale. Additionally, not having to manage other employees can also reduce stress and workload for the seller.

However, one potential downside of not having any additional employees is the limited capacity for growth. With only one person handling all aspects of the business, there may be a limit to how much work can be taken on and how many sales can be made. This could potentially hinder opportunities for expansion and increase revenue.

Ultimately, in this case, the buyer saw this lack of additional employees as a pro because it gave them control over their own growth. They could gradually scale up their business at a pace that worked for them without being constrained by existing staff or needing to hire more employees.

Step 4: Securing Financing

Laura and Tom decided to use a Home Equity Line of Credit (HELOC) and their cash savings to fund the acquisition. This approach allowed them to make an all-cash offer, facilitating a quick and smooth transaction.

Step 5: Negotiating the Deal

Laura and Tom negotiated a fair purchase price based on the business's current earnings, assets, and growth potential. Mark and Sarah, eager to move to Ohio and care for Mark's mother, were open to negotiation. The all-cash offer enabled a swift and uncomplicated closing process, benefiting both parties.

One key aspect of the deal was ensuring a seamless transition. Mark and Sarah agreed to provide training and support during the handover period, ensuring Laura and Tom could maintain the business's high standards and customer satisfaction.

Step 6: Transitioning into Ownership

To ensure a smooth transition, Laura and Tom spent the first few weeks shadowing Mark and Sarah, learning the business's intricacies, and meeting key clients and suppliers. This period was crucial for understanding the operational workflow and maintaining continuity.

An important part of the transition process was ensuring that Mark and Sarah could provide adequate support and guidance to Laura and Tom after they relocated to Ohio. Since the deal was closed quickly with an all-cash offer, Mark and Sarah sold their home and moved out of state shortly after the handover period. To facilitate a smooth and continuous transfer of knowledge and expertise, Mark and Sarah agreed to offer extended support virtually for six months after the sale. They communicated regularly with Laura and Tom via phone, email, and video calls, answering any questions and resolving any issues that arose. This arrangement helped Laura and Tom feel more confident and comfortable in running the business on their own while still benefiting from Mark and Sarah's experience and insights.

Laura focused on leveraging her marketing expertise to enhance client relationships and explore new business opportunities, while Tom provided financial oversight and strategic guidance.

Step 7: Implementing Growth Strategies

Once fully in control, Laura implemented several growth strategies:

- **Expanding Service Offerings:** Introduced new marketing services based on client demand and market trends.

- **Enhancing Online Presence:** Developed a comprehensive digital marketing strategy, including a new website, social media campaigns, and online client portals.

- **Growing the Team:** Hired additional marketing specialists and account managers to handle the increased workload and client base. Laura also created a mentorship program to foster employee development and retention.

Outcome

In just one year, Laura turned the marketing company into a flourishing enterprise. Her marketing expertise and community connections drove increased client satisfaction and revenue growth. The business's revenue doubled, and its market presence expanded significantly, establishing a robust new client base.

Laura's journey from a marketing executive to a successful business owner exemplifies the potential of strategic acquisition. By leveraging her skills, passion, and a well-thought-out plan, she achieved her dream of business ownership while providing a balanced and fulfilling life for her family.

3. Military Leader to Business Leader Transitioning from Service to Entrepreneurship

Buyer Background

Meet Jake Harrison, a dedicated Marine stationed in California. Throughout his military career, Jake harbored a dream of living in Texas, but he was never assigned to a station there. As his career progressed, his family grew to include his wife and six children, making California's high cost of living a challenge. At 38, Jake decided it was time to transition from his military career, seeking a new path that would provide growth opportunities and a better work-life balance. He believed that owning a business could offer the stability and flexibility he desired for his family.

Seller Background

The commercial landscaping business Jake found was based in Texas and owned by Tom Davis, whose father originally started the company. Tom had been a photographer, traveling across the country taking pictures of swimsuit models, but took over the business when his father fell ill. The company specialized in commercial landscaping, handling large plots of land such as oil and gas leases and new neighborhood developments. They were involved in one of the largest development projects in Texas, with contracts ensuring work for at least the next 5-10 years.

Despite the business's success and its prestigious client list, Tom decided to move on. Landscaping wasn't his passion, and he wanted to pursue other interests. He owned the land where the business operated, renting part of it to mobile homeowners, using a house on the property as the office (partially rented to a tenant), and housing all the business equipment on-site. Tom decided to sell the business but retain ownership of the land for ongoing rental income.

The Acquisition Journey

Jake's acquisition journey began with a clear vision: to leverage his leadership skills, strategic thinking, and desire for stability into owning and running a business. Here's a step-by-step look at how Jake navigated this transition.

Step 1: Identifying the Right Business

Jake knew his strengths lay in leadership, strategic planning, and operations management. He wanted a business where these skills would be crucial to success. After extensive research, he identified a profitable commercial landscaping business in Texas that matched his criteria. The business had a solid revenue stream, a well-established client base, and contracts ensuring future work.

Step 2: Evaluating the Business

Jake conducted thorough due diligence, which included:

- **Financial Analysis:** Reviewing the financial statements for the past five years to understand profitability, cash flow, and any outstanding debts.

- **Market Position:** Assessing the business's market position, customer base, and reputation.

- **Operational Efficiency:** Analyzing the business's operations, including equipment, maintenance schedules, and employee performance.

- **Growth Potential:** Identifying areas for growth, such as expanding services, increasing marketing efforts, and improving operational efficiency.

Step 3: Understanding the Business Structure

The commercial landscaping business had a well-organized structure, with experienced staff handling various operational aspects. Employees held Commercial Driver's Licenses (CDLs), allowing them to drive the equipment to job sites and operate it on-site. The team was largely self-sufficient, requiring minimal supervision. Additionally, the company had two finish-out crews dedicated to weed eating and clearing areas after the main landscaping work was done. This setup ensured efficient and high-quality service for their commercial clients, which included some of the top builders in the Dallas-Fort Worth (DFW) area. The existing contracts provided a stable revenue stream and long-term business prospects.

Step 4: Securing Financing

Jake recognized the need for additional financing to ensure sufficient working capital after the acquisition. He explored various financing options and ultimately secured an SBA loan with favorable terms, including a 10% down payment and a line of credit for working capital.

The decision to use the seller's bank was a strategic one, as Jake knew that this particular bank had a strong and positive history with the seller. By choosing to work with this top 5 bank, Jake leveraged the existing relationship between the bank and the seller, which helped create a smooth and efficient financing process.

Not only did this save time and effort on closing the deal, but it also gave Jake an advantage in negotiations. The seller may have been more inclined to offer better terms or rates due to their previous positive experiences with this bank.

By working with a reputable bank that had already financed previous vehicles for the seller, Jake could trust that they were reliable and trustworthy. This helped to ease any concerns or doubts about the financing process and instilled confidence in both parties.

Overall, choosing to use the seller's bank for financing was a smart move by Jake. It not only helped facilitate a swift closing of the deal but also strengthened his negotiating power and provided peace of mind for all involved.

Step 5: Negotiating the Deal

Jake negotiated a fair purchase price based on the business's current earnings, assets, and growth potential. Tom, eager to move on from the business, was open to negotiation. They agreed on a combination of an upfront payment and a seller-financed portion, with Jake acquiring the business and Tom retaining ownership of the land.

One key factor that helped Jake secure a favorable financing deal was the transfer of accounts receivable at closing. This arrangement meant that Jake would receive payments for the work already done by the business, providing him with additional working capital. Tom was willing to agree to this as he wanted to ensure the buyer's success and keep his father's legacy alive. He trusted Jake to honor the existing contracts and maintain the high standards of service that the business was known for. By transferring the accounts receivable, Tom demonstrated his confidence in Jake and his commitment to helping him succeed.

These factors helped Jake secure a smooth cash flow and maintain a good relationship with the seller. Jake appreciated Tom's guidance and support during the transition period and respected his decision to step back from the business. By renting the office space from Tom, Jake ensured a convenient location for the business operations.

Step 6: Transitioning into Ownership

To ensure a smooth transition, Jake spent the first few weeks shadowing Tom, learning the business's intricacies, and meeting key customers and suppliers. Tom provided additional training and agreed to be available for consultation in the future.

Looking around at the expansive plots being landscaped and the fleet of tractors in operation, Jake felt a sense of excitement and determination. He envisioned improvements, new markets to explore, and a legacy to build. With a deep breath, he embraced his new role, ready to lead the business to greater heights.

Step 7: Implementing Growth Strategies

Once fully in control, Jake implemented several growth strategies:

- **Expanding Services:** Introduced new landscaping services based on market demand and client feedback.
- **Enhancing Online Presence:** Developed a comprehensive digital marketing strategy, including a new website, social media campaigns, and online client portals.

- **Optimizing Operations:** Streamlined operations, improved equipment maintenance schedules, and enhanced employee training programs.

Outcome

Within a few years, Jake transformed the commercial landscaping business into a thriving enterprise. His leadership skills and strategic planning drove increased efficiency, customer satisfaction, and revenue growth. The business's revenue doubled, and its market presence expanded significantly, establishing a robust new client base.

Jake's journey from a military leader to a successful business owner exemplifies the potential of strategic acquisition. By leveraging his skills, passion, and a well-thought-out plan, he turned a new chapter in his professional life, achieving his dream of being his own boss while providing a better life for his family.

Chapter 11
GROW BABY GROW

Mergers and acquisitions (M&A) is the #1 growth strategy for entrepreneurs who want to scale their businesses, maximize their value, and create a lasting legacy. M&A allows you to tap into new markets, leverage existing assets, and generate a steady stream of cash flow that can fuel further expansion and innovation.

But don't just take our word for it. The numbers speak for themselves. According to a study by the Institute for Mergers, Acquisitions and Alliances (IMAA), M&A activity has been steadily increasing over the past four decades, reaching a record high of 49,849 deals worth $3.8 trillion in 2019. M&A is not only a popular strategy among large corporations, but also among small and medium-sized enterprises (SMEs), which accounted for 86% of all deals in 2019.

Why are acquisitions so prevalent among entrepreneurs of all sizes and sectors? Because they work. Research shows that M&A can generate significant value for both buyers and sellers, as well as for shareholders and stakeholders. A meta-analysis of 93 studies found that M&A has a positive impact on financial performance, operational efficiency, innovation, and market power.

In short, M&A is the #1 tool for entrepreneurs who want to grow their businesses, maximize their value, and create a lasting legacy. It's not a coincidence that some of the most successful entrepreneurs in history, such as Warren Buffett, Richard Branson, and Mark Zuckerberg, have used M&A as a key component of their growth strategies. By following their footsteps, you too can leverage the power of M&A to achieve your entrepreneurial goals and dreams.

Cash Flow for Legacy Building

When you acquire a business, you're not just buying assets, you're securing a stream of cash flow that, if managed astutely, can fund not only the growth of that business but also fuel other ventures and philanthropic activities that embody your values and vision. It's this cash flow that can be the bedrock on which your legacy is built.

Consider the potential of reinvesting this cash flow into the business to spur innovation, expand operations, or acquire complementary companies. Each of these actions can dramatically increase the value of the business and, by extension, the robustness of your legacy.

Alternatively, this cash flow can be channeled into creating a foundation that supports causes dear to your ethos, effectively imprinting your mark on the societal canvas. These philanthropic endeavors not only reflect your commitment to social responsibility but also ensure that your legacy is both felt and remembered.

But how do you ensure that this cash flow is put to its highest and best use? It begins with a meticulous analysis of the business's financial health and a strategic plan for its cash flow. This requires a clear understanding of the business's operational needs, growth opportunities, and potential risks.

Effective cash flow management is also about timing. Knowing when to dig, when to store, and when to sell is crucial. It's akin to the rhythm of a well-drilled mine, where each financial decision plays a role that contributes to the grand extraction of your legacy.

It's imperative to imbue your team with the vision of legacy building. Your employees, managers, and stakeholders must all grasp the importance of cash flow management in the context of legacy. When they do, every business decision is made not just for the quarter ahead but for the decades to come.

In this journey of legacy building, transparency and accountability are your allies. They engender trust among your stakeholders and ensure that the cash flow is managed with integrity. This trust is the currency of a lasting legacy, as valuable, if not more, than the financial gains it may yield.

It's also essential to adapt and evolve. The economic landscape is ever-changing, and a static approach to cash flow management can spell stagnation. A dynamic strategy that is responsive to market trends, technological advancements, and shifts in consumer behavior is key to ensuring that your legacy is not just durable but also relevant.

Legacy building through strategic cash flow utilization is a path less traveled, but it is one that can lead to unparalleled fulfillment. The businesses you acquire and the cash flow they generate are not just line items on a balance sheet; they are the gems from which your legacy will shine.

Ready, Set, Win!

Firstly, we have the strategy of meticulous prospecting. This is the cornerstone of any successful mining operation, where knowledge is power. It involves a deep dive into the geological, environmental, and regulatory facets of the target site. The devil is truly in the details here, and missing a beat can mean the difference between a lucrative vein and a costly mistake. By understanding every nuance of the land you intend to mine, you can make informed decisions that maximize yields and minimize risks.

The second strategy is cultural mining. It's not enough to dig up the gold and silver; successful acquisition must also extract the gems of corporate culture. This is where many miners hit a wall, as the human element of business is often the most resistant. Carving out a shared vision and aligning values across teams can turn a good vein into a great one. It ensures that once the ore has been refined, the real work of building a unified company can begin with all hands-on deck, drilling in the same direction.

The third strategy is post-merger integration planning. This is the blueprint for how two companies will operate as a single entity. It's a plan that touches every level of the organization, from the C-suite to customer service. It involves the integration of technology, processes, and people, and it must be both flexible and robust. Without a clear plan, the post-merger phase can be chaotic, eroding the value you sought to create. With it, you can hit the ground running, capturing efficiency and driving growth from day one.

Each strategy supports and enhances the others, creating a holistic approach to a transaction that can withstand the challenges and capitalize on the opportunities that such endeavors bring.

In implementing these strategies, it is critical to remember that while a deal can accelerate growth, they are not a panacea for all business woes. They require careful thought, meticulous planning, and unwavering commitment to see through. The best merger strategies are tailored to the unique circumstances of the deal and the companies involved. They consider not only the financial implications but also the human impact, the market dynamics, and the long-term vision for the combined entity.

There's a delicate balance to be struck between confidence and caution. Overzealousness can blind you to red flags, while undue hesitation can cause you to miss out on golden opportunities. Striking that balance is an art, honed through experience, instinct, and sometimes, a touch of luck.

Strategy I: Single Business Acquisition

When you acquire a business, it's like striking gold in a mine that opens up new veins of wealth. This isn't about prospecting with multiple small digs or incremental extraction. It's about making a calculated, bold move that places you in a new league. Think of it as a mining expedition where a single discovery can make you rich.

The essence of this strategy is to create a powerful impact with one decisive acquisition. It could be buying out a competitor, acquiring a company that allows you to offer a complete solution to your customers, or entering a new market with a well-established brand. What matters is that the business you acquire brings with it a substantial customer base, a reputable brand, or a unique product or service that can catapult you ahead of the competition.

Consider a tech company that has been steadily growing but is in a fiercely competitive market. Acquiring another tech firm with a unique intellectual property or a strong foothold in an untapped market can radically change its competitive dynamics. Suddenly, the company isn't just another player; it becomes a market leader.

The financial implications of such a move are equally significant. With the right acquisition, you could significantly increase your revenue streams and create economies of scale that reduce costs. This can lead to improved profit margins and a stronger balance sheet, making your business more attractive to investors and lenders.

There's also a human element to this strategy that cannot be ignored. Acquiring a business means bringing together different teams and cultures. It's about creating a new shared vision and harnessing the collective talents to drive the business forward. This human synergy can be the most potent outcome of a single business acquisition.

If you're looking for a business to acquire or invest in, you need to consider more than just the numbers and the market position. You need to find a business that aligns with your vision, values, and goals. A business that excites you and challenges you to grow. A business that fits your personality and lifestyle.

Choosing the right business can make all the difference. Although there are numerous choices, figuring out what is right for you is the bang for the buck. Here are some questions to ask yourself before you make a decision:

- **What are you passionate about?** What are your interests, hobbies, and skills? Do you have a specific problem that you want to solve or a gap that you want to fill in the market?

- **What are your strengths and weaknesses?** What are the areas that you excel in and the areas that you need to improve? Do you have the experience, knowledge, and network to run a successful business? Or do you need a partner or a mentor to guide you?

- **What are your financial goals and expectations?** How much capital do you have and how much are you willing to risk? How much revenue and profit do you expect to generate? How fast do you want to see a return on your investment?

- **What are your personal and professional goals?** How do you balance work and life? How much time and energy are you willing to devote to your business? How do you measure success and satisfaction?

- **What are the risks and opportunities involved?** What are the potential challenges and threats that you may face in the market? How do you mitigate them? What are the unique advantages and benefits that you can offer to your customers? How do you differentiate yourself from the competition?

By answering these questions, you can narrow down your options and focus on the businesses that suit your needs and preferences. Choosing the right business can make all the difference. It can be the key to unlocking your potential, fulfilling your dreams, and creating a lasting impact.

Let's also remember that with great power comes great responsibility. A larger business means more employees depending on your leadership, more customers expecting your best, and more stakeholders to answer to. It's a step that requires not just financial acumen but also leadership qualities that inspire and motivate.

Strategy II: Building a Portfolio

The rationale behind building a portfolio of businesses is rooted in the age-old wisdom of not putting all one's 'gold' in one basket. By spreading investments across different industries, sectors, or geographical locations, a savvy entrepreneur can shield their overall portfolio from the volatility that plagues individual markets. This mosaic of businesses can buffer against economic downturns, as the underperformance of one entity may be offset by the robust performance of another.

The acquisition of a variety of businesses is not a practice restricted to the titans of industry. It's a strategy accessible to the astute businessperson willing to diligently research, evaluate, and invest in companies with solid cash flows and growth potential.

One critical aspect to consider when building a business portfolio is the synergy between acquired companies. Synergy, in this context, refers to the potential additional value generated from combining businesses. For instance, if you own a chain of coffee shops, acquiring a bakery might provide cost advantages through the vertical integration of supply chains. This not only reduces dependency on external suppliers but also enhances control over the quality and pricing of the products offered.

Moreover, acquiring businesses that complement one another can lead to cross-promotion opportunities, shared customer bases, and the consolidation of administrative functions. These operational efficiencies can reduce costs and increase profitability. The goal is to create a self-sustaining ecosystem where each business supports and strengthens the others, ultimately leading to a sum greater than its parts.

Another vital element of this strategy is the concept of 'buying cash flow.' It's not just about acquiring assets; it's about investing in businesses that already have a proven track record of generating revenue. This approach minimizes the risk associated with startups or ventures that are yet to establish themselves in the market. By focusing on cash flow-positive businesses, you ensure a steady stream of income that can be reinvested to fuel further growth or weather unexpected financial challenges.

In implementing this strategy, one must also be vigilant about due diligence. Before adding a business to your portfolio, it's imperative to conduct a thorough analysis of its financial health, market position, competitive advantages, and growth prospects. This meticulous vetting process helps in identifying hidden risks and assessing the true value of the investment.

Furthermore, it's essential to have a robust management structure in place. Overseeing multiple businesses demands a significant amount of time and resources. As such, delegating responsibilities to competent managers who share your vision and have a vested interest in the success of the ventures is critical. This empowers you to maintain a strategic overview and focus on high-level decision-making, rather than being bogged down by day-to-day operations.

Building a portfolio of businesses is not a path devoid of challenges. It requires adaptability, resilience, and an unwavering commitment to continuous learning and improvement. Markets evolve, consumer preferences change, and what works today may not work tomorrow. Thus, staying informed, being proactive in the face of change, and having the flexibility to pivot when necessary are key to sustaining and growing your business portfolio.

Strategy III: Buy, Sell, Repeat

The beauty of this approach lies in its simplicity. You're not juggling multiple businesses simultaneously, but rather focusing all your effort and resources on one, making it the best it can be before moving on. It's a journey of immersion, learning, and transferring that knowledge into tangible improvements that increase the business's value.

Imagine stepping into a business that's performing moderately well. You see potential brimming beneath the surface. With a keen eye, you identify inefficiencies, areas for growth, and strategies to boost profitability. You implement changes, perhaps streamline operations, expand the customer base, or introduce new products or services. As the business flourishes under your guidance, you're not just improving a company; you're building a narrative of success that makes the business more attractive to potential buyers.

It's a process of extraction that you master, and when the final stage yields the most valuable ore, you offer it to the world. The business, now more profitable and efficient, is a gold mine for investors or entrepreneurs looking for their next opportunity. By selling it, you're not merely transferring ownership; you're delivering a treasure of improvement and the potential of continued success.

This strategy also allows you to specialize in a particular phase of business development. Some entrepreneurs thrive on the initial challenge of turning around a struggling business, while others find their stride in scaling operations to new heights. By sequentially buying and selling, you can focus on what you do best, honing your skills with each project.

The buy/sell approach can mitigate risks. Instead of being tied down to the fate of a single business for the long term, you can adapt and move on after each sale, staying agile in the face of market changes. You're not putting all your 'gold' in one basket but rather cultivating and then distributing them one by one.

The sequential buy and sell method is not just about financial gain—it's about personal and professional growth. With each business you buy, you learn new lessons, encounter different challenges, and develop a broader skill set. These experiences compound over time, shaping you into a more capable and nuanced businessperson.

This strategy does require a certain level of commitment and expertise. You need to understand the ins and outs of mergers and acquisitions, market valuations, and how to make a business attractive to buyers. It also demands patience and the willingness to sometimes ride out tough times before a business is ready to sell.

However, the rewards can be substantial. Each successful sale can fund the acquisition of a larger or more profitable mine, allowing you to increase your output and your income. It's the entrepreneurial equivalent of digging for gold, with each vein yielding a nugget that's more valuable than the last.

Choosing Your Path

How do you navigate this world with the grace of a seasoned diplomat and the acumen of a street-smart entrepreneur? It begins with a clear understanding of your objectives. Are you looking to acquire to grow your market share, diversify your offerings, or perhaps you're eyeing the technology that will catapult your operations into a new era? Maybe your goal is to merge with a peer to consolidate your position in a competitive market.

Next, assess your resources. Do you have the capital to pursue a major acquisition, or are you better off with a series of smaller, strategic deals that will add up to a significant impact? Your resources are not just monetary; they also include your team's skills, your operational efficiency, and your market reputation. Like a prospector surveying their land before digging, you must know the scope and scale of your assets before you plan your strategy.

The vision for success is where your strategy gains its most vibrant colors. It's the dream that keeps you awake at night, the future state that you can almost taste. It's the destination you're so passionately pursuing. Whether that vision is to become a market leader, to innovate relentlessly, or to provide exceptional value to your customers, it must be woven into every aspect of your M&A strategy. It's not just about the companies you acquire, but also about how you integrate them, the culture you cultivate, and the message you send to the market.

Choosing your path to victory in acquisition is not about following a trend or replicating another's success. It's a deeply personal journey that requires you to understand not only the terrain you're navigating but also the unique attributes of your own enterprise. It involves asking yourself tough questions and being willing to alter your course when the winds change. You must be a savvy miner who knows when to dig deeper, when to switch veins, and when to strike a deal.

Consider the case of a small tech startup with a revolutionary product. Their objective might be to get acquired by a larger player with the resources to bring their innovation to the masses. For them, the strategy may involve targeted networking, protecting their intellectual property fiercely, and proving their value in the market. On the other hand, a well-established corporation with a cash surplus might look to acquire startups to inject innovation into their product lines. Their strategy would differ, focusing on identifying potential acquisition targets, conducting thorough due diligence, and ensuring a smooth integration.

Your acquisition strategy is more than just a set of tactics. It's a reflection of your business's identity, aspirations, and ethos. It's about finding the right partners, creating synergies that multiply value, and navigating the post-acquisition landscape with a steady hand. It's about being nimble enough to pivot when necessary, yet steadfast in your pursuit of your end goals.

Acquisition can help you realize your vision for success more quickly and effectively. It is the best growth tool for any business, no matter the size or sector, and it can guide you to your goal with certainty and simplicity. Main Street Acquisition helps you dig deeper and strike gold with your acquisition. You can explore different veins and pick what suits your vision and capabilities. We congratulate you on your mining adventure.

AFTERWORD

In the ever-evolving landscape of entrepreneurship, moments of profound clarity often illuminate the path to success. One such moment occurred when I first encountered Xavier Egan's "Main Street Boom: Uncovering the Generational Gold Mine." With over 25 years of experience as an entrepreneur, I have seen the tides of business success rise and fall. Yet, the insights and strategies presented in this book resonate deeply with the essence of what drives true economic growth and individual prosperity.

Main Street businesses are the heartbeat of our economy, the hidden treasures that, when uncovered, reveal immense value and potential. Xavier Egan captures this sentiment with a masterful blend of research, real-world examples, and practical advice. His exploration of the dynamics that shape small businesses and their critical role in the broader economic landscape is both enlightening and inspiring. These businesses are not just numbers on a balance sheet; they are the lifeblood of our communities, driving innovation, creating jobs, and fueling local economies.

Reflecting on my own journey, I recall the pivotal moments that shaped my entrepreneurial path. From my early days learning about business in school to the practical experiences that honed my skills, each step reinforced my belief in the power of small-scale operations. My mother, who completed college when I was 20, and the early loss of my father at the age of 5, instilled in me a resilience and determination that have been crucial in navigating the complex world of business ownership. Egan's book delves into the essence of these lessons, offering a blueprint for success that is both accessible and actionable. His emphasis on the generational wealth transfer happening as Baby Boomers retire is a timely and crucial insight. This transition presents a massive opportunity for the younger generation to inherit and transform thriving businesses, continuing legacies and building new ones.

Throughout my career, I have witnessed firsthand the transformative power of strategic acquisitions and the importance of a well-rounded investor portfolio. Egan's insights into these areas provide a clear roadmap for aspiring entrepreneurs and seasoned investors alike. He addresses the allure and challenges of entrepreneurship, emphasizing the importance of cash flow, the pitfalls to avoid, and the strategies for growth and diversification.

What sets this book apart is its practical approach, grounded in real-world examples and case studies that illustrate the tangible benefits of well-executed business strategies. Egan's meticulous attention to detail and comprehensive coverage of topics make this book an invaluable resource for anyone looking to navigate the complexities of the business world.

As the founder of YSCO, a consulting firm dedicated to helping businesses achieve their goals, I have always emphasized the importance of strategic planning and execution. Xavier Egan's insights align perfectly with this philosophy, offering valuable guidance on building a strong, sustainable business foundation.

In conclusion, "Main Street Boom: Uncovering the Generational Gold Mine" is more than just a book; it is a testament to the enduring power of entrepreneurship and a roadmap for future success. Xavier Egan's wisdom and experience shine through every page, providing a wealth of knowledge that is both profound and practical. I wholeheartedly support this work and the incredible potential it holds for entrepreneurs at every stage of their journey. Whether you are just starting out or looking to expand your business, this book offers the tools and insights you need to uncover your own generational gold mine.

Sam Mattox, Founder & Managing Director
YSCO

AUTHOR'S NOTE

Congratulations to you on completing this book!

"Main Street Boom" is not just a book—it's a blueprint for achieving enduring success through the power of acquisitions. Whether you're a seasoned entrepreneur or just starting out, I can provide insights and practical advice to guide you towards making informed, strategic decisions that can transform your business and secure your financial future.

At the core of every thriving community lies a strong and sustainable economy. As an advocate for positive change, I am deeply committed to uplifting others as well as building better community economics through my unwavering dedication and determination.

My passion for creating a more prosperous society stems from my belief that economic stability is the key to empowering individuals, families, and businesses alike. I firmly believe that by working together with local leaders, businesses, and residents, we can create an environment where everyone has access to opportunities for growth and success.

Ready to Discover Your Hidden Wealth on Main Street?

If yes, then now is the perfect time to contact me to take your journey to the next step. Let's discover your gold mine together. My expert team and I will advise on Buy and Sell side Business Technology, and Real Estate transactions; providing solutions and partners across all asset classes.

For media appearances and public speaking inquiries, please email contact@xavieregan.co.

Best,

XAVIER EGAN
President of Mergers & Acquisitions
+1 (817) 609-4561
www.xavieregan.co

Follow me on LinkedIn, IG, Facebook and Twitter! @XavierEganDealMaker

DEFINITIONS

Before we delve into the details of how to choose your path to acquisition, we want to clarify some key terms that we will use throughout this guide. These definitions are not meant to be exhaustive or academic, but rather practical and relevant for the aspiring entrepreneur who wants to grow their business through acquisition. We have selected these terms based on our experience and expertise in helping Main Street businesses achieve their goals. We hope that by explaining these concepts in simple and accessible language, we can help you gain more clarity and confidence as you embark on your mining adventure.

Acquisition: The act of obtaining ownership of a company or asset.

Assets: Resources owned by a business that have economic value.

Balance Sheet: A financial statement that summarizes a company's assets, liabilities, and shareholders' equity.

Benchmarking: Comparing business processes and performance metrics to industry bests and best practices.

Brand Equity: The value of a brand, measured by the extent of customer loyalty and the prices customers are willing to pay.

Business Broker: A person or firm that assists buyers and sellers of privately held businesses in the buying and selling process.

Business Valuation: The process of determining the economic value of a business or company.

Buy-Sell Agreement: A legally binding agreement between co-owners of a business that determines what happens if one of the co-owners dies or otherwise leaves the business.

Capital: Financial assets or the financial value of assets, such as cash.

Cash Flow: The total amount of money being transferred into and out of a business.

Commercial Loan: A debt-based funding arrangement between a business and a financial institution.

Competitive Advantage: A condition or circumstance that puts a company in a favorable or superior business position.

Corporate Executive: A high-ranking officer in a corporation, typically in charge of overall operations and management.

Customer Acquisition Cost (CAC): The cost associated with convincing a customer to buy a product/service.

Disruption: Innovation that creates a new market and value network, eventually disrupting existing markets and displacing established market leaders.

Due Diligence: The investigation or exercise of care that a reasonable business or person is expected to take before entering into an agreement or contract.

Earnings Before Interest, Taxes, Depreciation, and Amortization (EBITDA): A measure of a company's overall financial performance.

Entrepreneurial Ecosystem: The social and economic environment affecting the local/regional entrepreneurship.

Equity: The value of shares issued by a company.

Exit Strategy: A planned approach to terminating a situation in a way that will maximize benefit or minimize damage.

Financial Statement: Formal records of the financial activities and position of a business, person, or other entity.

Franchise: The authorization granted by a company to an individual or group enabling them to carry out specified commercial activities.

Freemium: A pricing strategy by which a product or service is provided free of charge, but money (premium) is charged for additional features.

Fundability: The likelihood that a business will be able to secure funding.

Goodwill: An intangible asset that arises when a buyer acquires an existing business.

Growth Strategy: A plan of action to increase the size and profitability of a business.

Incubator: A company that helps new and startup companies to develop by providing services such as management training or office space.

Initial Public Offering (IPO): The first time that the stock of a private company is offered to the public.

Intellectual Property: A category of property that includes intangible creations of the human intellect.

Intrapreneurship: The act of behaving like an entrepreneur while working within a large organization.

Inventory: The raw materials, work-in-progress goods, and finished goods considered to be the portion of a business's assets that are ready or will be ready for sale.

Leverage: The use of various financial instruments or borrowed capital to increase the potential return of an investment.

Liabilities: The company's legal debts or obligations that arise during the course of business operations.

Limited Liability Company (LLC): A corporate structure in the United States whereby the owners are not personally liable for the company's debts or liabilities.

Market Analysis: A quantitative and qualitative assessment of a market.

Market Penetration: The act of gaining a higher market share in an existing market.

Merger: The combination of two or more companies into a single entity.

Monopoly: The exclusive possession or control of the supply of or trade in a commodity or service.

Net Income: A company's total earnings (or profit).

Non-Disclosure Agreement (NDA): A legal contract that protects confidential information.

Omnichannel: A multichannel approach to sales that seeks to provide customers with a seamless shopping experience.

Operational Efficiency: The capability of an enterprise to deliver products or services to its customers in the most cost-effective manner possible while still ensuring the high quality of its products, service, and support.

Partnership: A business organization in which two or more individuals manage and operate the business.

Pitch Deck: A brief presentation, often created using PowerPoint, used to provide your audience with a quick overview of your business plan.

Portfolio: A range of investments held by a person or organization.

Private Equity: Capital that is not listed on a public exchange.

Profit Margin: A measure of profitability calculated as net income divided by revenue.

Product Lifecycle: The progression of a product through four stages: introduction, growth, maturity, and decline.

Pro Forma: Financial statements based on hypothetical scenarios for planning purposes.

Public Company: A company whose shares are traded freely on a stock exchange.

Return on Investment (ROI): A measure used to evaluate the efficiency or profitability of an investment.

Revenue: The income generated from normal business operations.

Risk Management: The process of identifying, assessing, and controlling threats to an organization's capital and earnings.

Scalability: The capacity to be changed in size or scale.

Securities: Financial instruments that hold some type of monetary value.

Share Buyback: A company buying back its shares from the marketplace.

Shareholder: An individual or institution that owns shares in a company.

Stakeholder: A person with an interest or concern in a business.

Startup: A company in the first stages of operations.

Stock Market: The aggregation of buyers and sellers of stocks, which represent ownership claims on businesses.

Subsidiary: A company controlled by another company.

Supply Chain: The sequence of processes involved in the production and distribution of a commodity.

SWOT Analysis: A strategic planning technique used to identify strengths, weaknesses, opportunities, and threats.

Target Market: A particular group of consumers identified as the recipients of a particular marketing message.

Taxation: The system by which a government takes money from people and spends it on public services.

Trade Secret: A type of intellectual property comprising formulas, practices, processes, designs, instruments, patterns, or compilations of information that have independent economic value.

Transaction: An instance of buying or selling something.

Turnaround: The process of making a company profitable again.

Upsell: A sales technique aimed at persuading the customer to purchase more expensive items, upgrades, or other add-ons.

Valuation: The analytical process of determining the current (or projected) worth of an asset or a company.

Venture Capital: Financing that investors provide to startup companies and small businesses that are believed to have long-term growth potential.

Vertical Integration: The combination in one company of two or more stages of production normally operated by separate companies.

Working Capital: The capital of a business which is used in its day-to-day trading operations.

Yield: The income return on an investment.

Zoning: The legislative process for dividing land into zones for different uses.

REFERENCES

1. U.S. Small Business Administration. (n.d.). *Small business GDP: Update 2002-2010*. Retrieved from https://www.sba.gov/sites/default/files/rs390tot_0.pdf - Mentioned in Chapter 1: Contribution of small businesses to GDP. (p. 5)

2. U.S. Small Business Administration. (2022). *2022 Small Business Profile*. Retrieved from https://cdn.advocacy.sba.gov/wp-content/uploads/2022/08/30114129/2022-Small-Business-Profiles-All.pdf - Mentioned in Chapter 1: Percentage of businesses in the U.S. that are small businesses. (p. 6)

3. U.S. Bureau of Labor Statistics. (2022). *Employment by industry, monthly changes*. Retrieved from https://www.bls.gov - Mentioned in Chapter 1: Employment statistics for small businesses. (p. 8)

4. National Federation of Independent Business. (2023). *Small Business Economic Trends*. Retrieved from https://www.nfib.com - Mentioned in Chapter 2: Economic impact of generational wealth transfer on small businesses. (p. 18)

5. Deloitte. (2022). *The ripple effect of generational wealth transfer*. Retrieved from https://www2.deloitte.com - Mentioned in Chapter 2: Statistics on generational wealth transfer. (p. 19)

6. Harvard Business Review. (2021). *The new M&A playbook*. Retrieved from https://hbr.org - Mentioned in Chapter 3: Strategies for investors. (p. 27)

7. Bloomberg. (2023). *Small business funding and loans*. Retrieved from https://www.bloomberg.com - Mentioned in Chapter 6: Fundability and navigating lending. (p. 45)

8. American Institute of Certified Public Accountants. (2022). *Business valuation guide*. Retrieved from https://www.aicpa.org - Mentioned in Chapter 7: Identifying deal partners. (p. 52)

9. Forbes. (2023). *Cash flow management for small businesses*. Retrieved from https://www.forbes.com - Mentioned in Chapter 11: Cash flow strategies. (p. 89)

10. The Wall Street Journal. (2023). *The rise of small business acquisitions*. Retrieved from https://www.wsj.com - Mentioned in Chapter 9: Benefits of acquisition. (p. 78)

www.ingramcontent.com/pod-product-compliance
Lightning Source LLC
Chambersburg PA
CBHW020339010526
44119CB00035B/452/J